Christmas
with Southern Living
1993

Compiled and Edited by
Vicki Ingham

Oxmoor House.

Library of Congress Catalog Card
   Number: 84-63032
ISBN: 0-8487-1133-5
ISSN: 0747-7791
Manufactured in the United States of America
First Printing

Editor-in-Chief: Nancy J. Fitzpatrick
Senior Homes Editor: Mary Kay Culpepper
Senior Editor, Editorial Services: Olivia Kindig Wells
Director of Manufacturing: Jerry Higdon
Art Director: James Boone

Christmas with Southern Living 1993

Editor: Vicki L. Ingham
Assistant Editor: Dondra G. Parham
Contributing Editor: Heidi Tyline King
Recipe Editor: Kaye Adams, Test Kitchens
   Director and Recipe Editor, *Southern Living*
   magazine
Editorial Assistants: Catherine S. Corbett,
   Karen Brechin
Copy Chief: Mary Jean Haddin
Assistant Copy Editor: L. Amanda Owens
Copy Assistant: Leslee Rester Johnson
Designer: Carol Middleton
Senior Photographer: John O'Hagan
Photostylist: Katie Stoddard
Production Manager: Rick Litton
Associate Production Manager: Theresa L. Beste
Production Assistant: Marianne Jordan
Artist: Barbara Ball

Introduction 1

Christmas Around The South 2

Holiday Traditions 22

Contents

Introduction

Southerners really do have a special knack for celebrating Christmas well—some folks say we've been doing it since 1607, when Captain John Smith and his men marked the day by inviting members of the Powhatan Confederacy to share a meal with them in Jamestown, Virginia. Later, Southern states were the first to make Christmas Day a legal holiday: Louisiana and Arkansas put it on the books in 1831, and Alabama followed suit in 1836.

For a closer look at how Southerners used to celebrate, see "Christmas Around the South," where we visit Winterthur, a museum in Delaware, and Old City Park in Dallas. And to experience Christmas in the two states that first made the holiday official, we go to Natchitoches, Louisiana, and Eureka Springs, Arkansas.

Food, friends, and faith were the substance of early Southern celebrations, and that's still true today. In fact, Christmas is the high season for giving and attending parties. Whether your style of entertaining is casual or formal, you'll find in the following pages recipes, party ideas, and decorations to inspire you.

If you like to have all of your friends over at the same time in a large, informal gathering, a buffet is the way to go. That's the choice of two Atlanta shopkeepers who invite clients, employees, and friends to join them at their weekend retreat in Highlands, North Carolina. For neighbors on a Florida island, a progressive party makes entertaining easier for everyone, while a group of friends in South Carolina favors a potluck feast for their daylong reunion.

If you prefer smaller, more formal parties, take a look at the first story in "Celebrations from the Kitchen." The staff of the *Southern Living* Test Kitchens has developed a delicious menu for an elegant seated dinner, along with a tablescape that features handsome boxwood topiaries. You can make these yourself by following our step-by-step instructions.

Decorations are, of course, the stage setting for holiday gatherings. You'll find lots of good ideas for decorations, and to help you adapt and re-create some of them more easily, we are introducing a new section called "Christmas Workroom." Look for it at the back of the book, following the recipes.

Christmas
Around the South

4

Winterthur Weaves
A Holiday Tale

*I*f your image of an old-fashioned Christmas includes a floor-to-ceiling tree with gifts beneath, stockings on the mantel, and carolers singing outside, you can thank the Victorians. They introduced many of the Christmas customs that we cherish today. Prior to the Victorian era, however, Southern celebrations—at least for the planter class—consisted of going to church, and then visiting neighboring plantations for an elaborate, three- or four-course meal and maybe some dancing or hunting.

That's the sort of thing you'll learn when you visit Winterthur in Wilmington, Delaware, during the holidays. This museum, formerly the home of Henry Francis du Pont, houses the nation's foremost collection of American decorative arts. Du Pont collected furniture, textiles, silver, porcelain, pewter, and paintings for more than four decades.

Above: Colored jellies displayed on a footed glass tazza form an edible centerpiece. Such jellies, made by boiling bone marrow to yield clear gelatin, showed off a hostess's culinary skill.

Paneling from a 1744 Maryland plantation house and 18th-century Philadelphia furniture provide the setting for a colonial three-course holiday dinner. Christmas was the big social season in the 1700s; celebrations focused on food rather than decorations or gifts.

Above: In the last two decades of the 18th century, long dining tables became fashionable, as did French centerpieces called plateaux. *George Washington had his European agents acquire one of these raised mirrors for him, along with a set of ornaments that included porcelain figurines and vases.*

To create appropriate settings for the objects, he rescued paneling, mantels, and other architectural features from old houses along the East Coast and had them installed in his rambling mansion. In 1951, he opened the house to the public.

For Yuletide at Winterthur, the museum staff decorates 20 of the rooms to illustrate customs drawn from two centuries of American holiday celebrations. Violet Riegel, projects coordinator in the Museum Education and Public Programs Division, spends about eight months each year researching and developing new vignettes for the rooms. All of the displays are historically documented through prints, paintings, or diary accounts, so each room offers an accurate and illuminating image of the past.

In the 1700s, for example, a table crowded with food was a mark of status, and guests were more impressed by abundance and appearance than by taste or nutrition. The display in the Marlboro Room (see page 4) re-creates the kind of holiday dinner that might have been served at Wye, a plantation on Maryland's Eastern Shore. Dishes, arranged in a symmetrical pattern, included rabbit, doves, oysters, gooseberry tarts, beaten biscuits, and plum pudding. The *pièce de résistance* was a pheasant pie, a meat dish covered with pastry and decorated with a pastry head and real tail feathers.

Documents from the du Pont family archives inspired the Empire Parlor vignette (page 8), which presents an early 19th-century musicale. Most well-bred young people played at least one instrument, and musicales were a popular way to spend a sociable evening. The program could be either informal or more sophisticated, like the one at E. I. du Pont's home in Delaware on December 18, 1823. It included solos and duets on piano and flute, popular French and American songs, and a full-band rendition of the opera *Don Juan*.

6

Evergreen swags emphasize the graceful lines of this free-hanging staircase, which was originally in Montmorenci, a North Carolina house built in 1822.

Above: This vignette illustrates an evening musicale, a popular way to entertain in the early 19th century. Guides discuss each room display as well as Winterthur's remarkable collection of antiques.

"An 1860 Christmas" (right) shows off high-style Belter furniture as well as the American innovation of floor-to-ceiling Christmas trees. The tree that was introduced in the early 19th century by German immigrants sat on a table. Carved and painted Noah's arks with their cargo of animals also came to this country from Germany. They were called "Sunday toys" because, thanks to their biblical message, they were the only ones that didn't have to be put away on the Sabbath.

More than 26,000 people tour Yuletide at Winterthur each year. (To find out how to join them, see page 156.) It's a wonderful opportunity to learn some holiday history and to see American Christmases past come to life. 🍎

Right: These high-style Victorian chairs, made in Baltimore, are part of a set in which each chair is carved with the head of a literary or historical figure. A tree decorated with gifts and a Noah's ark beneath reflect 19th-century Christmas customs transplanted from Germany.

8

Yuletide in Old Dallas

Ice pelted the windows of Millermore, but the St. Mark's Boys Choir sang anyway. The choir entertained a tiny group that gamely braved the storm to attend Christmas at Millermore in City Park. That was 1972, says Judith Farris, former president of the Guild of the Dallas County Heritage Society. There were only three historic buildings in the park at that time. Now, 21 years later, more than 35 structures form an open-air museum known as Old City Park, and the Christmas celebration called Candlelight is its biggest fund-raising event.

The park presents the architectural and cultural history of North Central Texas from 1840 to

Above: Millermore, the largest surviving antebellum mansion in Dallas, was moved to City Park in 1967. It was the first of more than 35 historic structures to be brought to the site to create Old City Park, an open-air museum of North Central Texas architectural and cultural history.

1910. At Christmas, over a thousand candles line the paths and illuminate the buildings, and the entire complex is filled with the sights and sounds of the season.

Structures include a railroad depot and hotel, a section house (home to members of the crew that maintained the railroad track), a church, a school, stores, and examples of domestic architecture that range from simple log cabins to turreted and gabled Victorian houses.

In December community groups adopt about half of the buildings and work with museum curators and the Candlelight Committee to design appropriate decorations. Old newspaper accounts, oral tradition, early photographs, and magazines supply clues to decorating customs. Curators note that the arrival of the railroad in the 1870s brought a dramatic change in Texas Christmas decorations—Christmas trees became popular and, for the first time, tinsel and blown-glass ornaments could be purchased. Jewish, African-American, and Mexican holiday traditions are also featured in some of the buildings.

Entertainment is continuous during Candlelight. At any given moment, ballerinas might be pirouetting on Main Street, a harpist playing at Millermore, a high school choir singing in the church, and a glee club caroling in the schoolhouse. There are also storytellers, craft demonstrations, and a chance to talk with Santa. It's a delightful way to spend a December evening. And if luck holds, you shouldn't have to worry about ice storms—there hasn't been one in early December since 1972. 🍂

Top right: Musicians perform throughout the park during the Candlelight festival, which is held on the first two weekends in December. To find out where to write for more information about scheduled events, see page 156.

Center right: Budding ballerinas perform on a temporary stage set up across from the general merchandise stores. The General Store would have served both farmers and townspeople. The store to the left is now the museum gift shop.

Above: Across from Millermore is an 1880s-style bandstand, where Santa and Mrs. Claus receive little visitors.

11

A Parade Is Only the Beginning

Natchitoches (pronounced, roughly, *Naka-dish*) has several claims to fame. Founded in 1714, it's the oldest European settlement in the Louisiana Purchase, a vast territory that was added to the United States in 1803. More recently, Hollywood has come to town to film *The Horse Soldiers*, *Steel Magnolias*, and *Man in the Moon*. But the event that really draws the crowds is the annual Christmas Festival, complete with a parade, fireworks, and thousands of colored lights.

Listed as one of the top 20 events in the region by the Southeast Tourism Society, the Christmas Festival has been lighting up the riverfront since 1927. Natchitoches is about halfway between Shreveport and Alexandria, so it draws folks from a wide area. On the first Saturday in December, the historic district closes to traffic for the day, and by midmorning throngs of holiday visitors—nearly 150,000 of them—fill the streets. A crafts fair and nonstop performances at an outdoor stage offer diversion, and there are dozens of food stalls where you can get everything from gumbo to barbecue to the famous meat pies that are a Natchitoches specialty. By early afternoon, people begin to find their places along the parade route, which starts at Northwestern State University and ends on Front Street, along the river's edge.

When the parade ends, the riverbank quickly becomes a crazy quilt of blankets and tarpaulins, as families stake out spots for viewing the fireworks. Afterwards, with a flip of the switch, the lights come on. Strings of old-fashioned, multicolored Christmas tree bulbs form a canopy over Front Street, line Second Street, and outline the bridges across the Cane River, earning the town its designation as the City of Lights. Illuminated displays designed and built by the city's former chief electrician, Charles Solomon, line the riverbank opposite Front Street.

The festival kicks off a month of activities in Natchitoches. There are tours of historic homes and plantations, nightly entertainment at the riverfront, boat rides on the river, and carriage rides through town.

The marching band from Northwestern State University leads the Christmas parade through Natchitoches. More than 120 groups from all over north and central Louisiana participate, including high school bands and drill teams, the Shriners, horseback riding clubs, pageant winners, and area businesses that sponsor floats of all kinds.

13

Above: Fireworks light up the sky over the Cane River, bringing to a spectacular close the one-day Christmas Festival. But it's just the beginning of a month of holiday activities.

Left: Shimmering reflections in the river enhance the magical effect of illuminated displays called set pieces and colored lights outlining the bridge.

At the Laureate House, visitors enjoy a tour with a twist: each room is the setting for part of *A Visit from St. Nicholas,* enacted by friends and pupils of owner Martha Wynn.

"We just wanted something unique," says Martha, an elementary school principal. "And having children involved at Christmas—what could be more appropriate?"

The house was built in 1840. It served as an in-town residence for the owners, who lived on a plantation and would come into town to shop and conduct business.

Outside of town, the road follows the wrinkled course of the Cane River, taking you past plantation houses surrounded by flat fields. Several houses open for tours year-round are especially festive at Christmas—one is Magnolia, which has been in the same family since the original French

Opposite top left: Martha Wynn and friends greet visitors at the Laureate House, where the tour features a production of A Visit from St. Nicholas. *Martha's red dress is a period costume handmade by Debbie LaCaze, who is the second from the left.*

Opposite top right: Clement Moore's poem comes to life, thanks to the thespian talents of Ryan Horton, assistant pastor at Martha's church, and children from her school.

Opposite bottom: Papa in his cap describes to appreciative visitors his unexpected encounter with the Jolly Old Elf.

Top right: The plantation home of Magnolia, like other Creole cottages in the area, is raised on brick piers and has galleries across the front and back. One of only two National Bicentennial Farms west of the Mississippi, Magnolia has been in the same family and in continuous operation for 240 years.

Bottom right: The wide center hall serves as a reception area. Furnished with Empire, Victorian, and early Louisiana pieces (some of which are original to the house), Magnolia is a private home, but is open for tours every afternoon.

Above: An old oil jar holds a seasonal arrangement of pine, cotton, pyracantha, and yaupon holly.

land grant was made in 1753. The house, built in the 1830s, was burned in the Civil War and rebuilt in 1896. Betty Hertzog, who grew up there, continues to live in the house and, with her cousin, runs the 2,192-acre plantation.

To say that Natchitoches is one big family is not just a figure of speech. A walking-tour guide notes that "one-third of the town's population are kin folks," and the family ties extend to the plantations, too. That's probably one reason that the festival seems a lot like a reunion. But even if it's your first time to attend, you'll feel welcome. "Everybody here is glad you came and they want you to come back," says Richard Ware, former head of the town's tourist commission. "They'll do anything for you, anything you need." 🌿

Take a Shopping Holiday in Eureka Springs

*E*ureka Springs, Arkansas, welcomes Christmastime tourists with hospitality, charming architecture, and a host of shopping opportunities. Townspeople outline the rooflines of downtown buildings with white lights and festoon the storefronts with fresh greenery. It's peaceful and pretty, and the residents are gracious and mannerly. When there is snow, the town is magical.

Jim Nelson owns a leather shop in Eureka. "This is a very humanly scaled place—narrow streets, small shops," he says. "People may not know why they like the place, but I think it's because they can relate to it more easily than to larger and newer tourist towns."

The streets don't cross in this town: They all merge. Likewise, the residents—artists, craftsmen,

Above: Eureka Springs has become a haven for artists, craftspeople, and entrepreneurs. Dolloped with snow as soft as whipped cream, East Mountain in December affords glimpses of the town hidden at other times of the year by magnificent foliage.

19

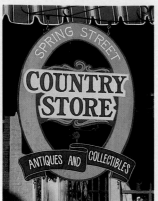

and those captivated by the resort town's character—have joined together to guard the architecture, both august and average, of Eureka's gingerbread past. Cottages constructed with steep gables and lacy millwork stand alongside grand limestone bath houses, municipal buildings, and hotels.

Just a day's drive from Tulsa, Memphis, St. Louis, or Dallas, Eureka Springs puts visitors into a setting like that of a Victorian novel. Christmas shopping along the winding and climbing streets is not an endurance contest. You can park your car and conquer your gift list on foot. Nestled into the hillside are shops offering folk art, fine art, pottery, dolls, jewelry, toys, antiques, kaleidoscopes, fudge, and more. Wares are homemade, handmade, or imported from abroad to fill this merry Ozark marketplace.

Since the town's founding in 1870, the only industry has been tourism. "Visitors are important to all our merchants," says Susan Morrison, artist and gallery owner. "People

Above: In Eureka you literally browse "up and down" through a change of elevation. Some 230 pedestrian-friendly streets lead visitors from the Crescent Hotel down Spring Street through the Historic Shopping District with hundreds of fun stops and shops in between. Wear comfortable walking shoes for a perfect shopping experience.

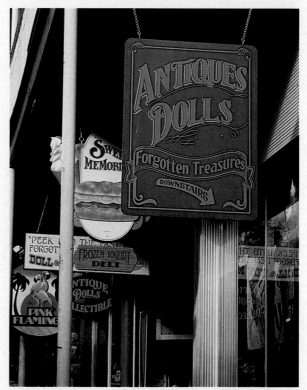

Above: Window shopping or gourmet dining may be your entertainment after the stores close for the night. Or you may opt for a lively country music show or choose a seat at the outdoor amphitheater to see The Great Passion Play. *During the holiday season, the play features a reenactment of the Nativity story.*

are amazed that shopkeepers are so delighted to see them."

Accommodations are plentiful and varied, from inns, cabins, and cottages to bed and breakfasts. It is a warm and cozy hideaway from the hectic pace of urban yuletide. Sara Armellini of Spring Wind Gallery boasts, "We're not different from what we are the rest of the year, but at Christmas Eureka Springs is different from the rest of the world." ❦

Above: The fresh smell of evergreen, the luminous glow of Christmas lights, and the wonder of decorated store windows dress Eureka Springs for the season. Family-run businesses make Christmas shopping here an old-fashioned pleasure. You can plan your visit to include the annual Christmas House Tour or a neighborhood caroling contest.

SHOPPING GETAWAYS

To help you plan your Christmas gifting trip, scout our list of shopping possibilities. Charming settings, great dining, and an eclectic offering of wares make each a holiday adventure. Write the information bureau provided for all the details.

Eureka Springs, Arkansas ❦ Step into a Christmas novel when you shop in this Ozark Mountain town. Contact the Chamber of Commerce at P.O. Box 551, Eureka Springs, AR 72632.

Franklin, Tennessee ❦ Architecturally rich Historic Downtown Franklin sparkles like a Christmas jewel with parades, merry merchants, and a lively Victorian street festival. Contact Williamson County Tourism at P.O. Box 156, Franklin, TN 37065-0156.

Ellicott City, Maryland ❦ This 200-year-old mill town decks historic Main Street with wreaths and Christmas shopping cheer. Contact the Howard County Tourism Council at P.O. Box 9, Ellicott City, MD 21041.

Dillsboro, North Carolina ❦ Find lots of locally made crafts for sale in this peaceful, tiny Smoky Mountain town. Contact the Jackson County Chamber of Commerce at 18 North Central St., Sylva, NC 28779.

Spring, Texas ❦ Just 20 minutes from the heart of Houston, Old Town offers small town Texas hospitality and specialty shops galore. Contact Old Town Spring Association at 123 E. Midway, Spring, TX 77373.

Holiday Traditions

The potpourris at the Texas General Store are some of the most fragrant ones you'll find. Joy and her daughter use natural oils and are always experimenting to develop new combinations of scents, textures, and colors, so that the potpourris are as pretty as they are aromatic.

From Texas, Natural Wonders

The garlands, swags, and wreaths at Joy Jowell's Texas General Store are different from most of the other dried flower-and-fruit decorations you'll see. "We use what we find in nature," she explains. "We're out there gathering things like bladderpod, a beautiful little bean that looks stunning in a wreath. People come into the shop and ask 'Where do you find these things?' I tell them, 'Walk one-half block away from here and you'll see it.' People are not used to seeing what's there. But once you have eyes to see, you're a danger on the road!"

To collect the wild plants and seedpods, she has an unusual crew of gatherers around the state—a bank president and his wife, for example, harvest clover in East Texas, and a biologist and his wife gather bee balm near Fredericksburg.

"When we gather, we follow the rule of three," explains Joy. "One for us, one for the birds and insects, and one for the Master Gardener to sow for the next year." So if there are three milkweed plants, Joy takes seedpods from only one. "We never strip the land bare," she says.

Of course, she uses garden flowers, too—acres of them are grown for her in California, and she air-dries them in the shop and at her home. Agricultural plants come from local farmers.

Joy credits her mother for teaching her to find beauty in unexpected places. In La Mesa, Texas, where she grew up, the dry, sandy soil supported tumbleweed instead of trees, and her uncles farmed dryland cotton. "We were poor in money, but wealthy in land and the garden and all of that," recalls Joy. "Mother would make up occasions and we would decorate the house." For materials, they collected grasses, vines, wildflowers, and berries and made creative use of what was available.

"The land has been good, the blessings have been many," says Joy of her 12 years in this business. "It's fun to make a living the way I do." She has a deep appreciation for the earth's bounty and tries to be a faithful steward of it, even as her floral designs celebrate its unexpected wonders. 🍎

Above: The Texas General Store is filled with distinctive folk art and unique gifts. "We work hard to find unusual things," says Joy.

Top: Joy Jowell combines dried flowers with common grasses and seedpods to create original and distinctive decorations that stand out at Christmas—or any time of year.

CRAFT A CHRISTMAS GARLAND

The yard-long kitchen garlands that Joy Jowell sells at the Texas General Store are based on the colonial practice of stringing dried herbs to hang in the kitchen. The cook would pinch off a bay leaf or a sprig of thyme or rosemary as needed and add it to the soup or stew. Joy's garlands are purely decorative, however, and her "swaggers" take great pride in executing the complex patterns that make them up. Here Joy shows how to assemble such a swag. To order supplies, see Resources, page 156.

Materials:
drill and ¼" or ⅜" drill bit
30 (4") cinnamon sticks
large-eyed needle and carpet thread
1 pound of bay leaves
24 dried apple slices
22 bunches of canella berries
3 dried pomegranates
jute twine

1. With a ¼" or ⅜" drill bit, drill a hole through center of each cinnamon stick.

2. Using a needle and carpet thread doubled to measure 40", string 3 cinnamon sticks onto thread. Leave a knotted loop at end for tying on a jute hanger. Carefully work the needle through center of a stack of bay leaves.

3. Continue adding materials in a regular pattern, alternating bay leaves and canella berries and adding dried apple slices, pomegranates, and cinnamon sticks, as shown here. To attach berries, align stems of 2 bunches so that berries extend in opposite directions; hold stems tightly against bay leaves and wrap with carpet thread. Secure with a knot before adding next stack of bay leaves.

4. To hang the garland, tie off thread at the end of the garland, make a knotted loop, and tie jute through the loop at each end.

Above: These heirloom plates are actually new creations in decoupage under glass. Choice papers are snipped, and then images are compiled to create a collage. The Victorian flavor of Rosemary Williams's holiday designs makes the plates and teacups desirable Christmas collectibles.

Old-World Images Serve Up Collectible Charm

Rosemary Williams of Mountain Brook, Alabama, uses every scrap of beautiful paper she can find—postcards, greeting cards, and wrapping paper—to decorate holiday plates that are a clever adaptation of the European art of decoupage.

Traditional decoupage was developed in the 18th century to imitate hand-painted oriental lacquerware. The technique refers to the process of decorating wood, metal, or glass with cut paper and applying as many as 20 coats of varnish over the motifs, with repeated sanding to produce a smooth, lustrous finish.

Rosemary, however, takes a different approach to the art. First, she builds an intricate collage from independent paper elements: Her goal is to create the illusion of a single image from many separate pieces. She trims figures out of postcards and wrapping paper and meticulously fits the paper edges together like a jigsaw puzzle. Rosemary says, "It's a challenge to cut things out in such a way that the seams disappear."

Then she glues the composition to the back of a clear glass plate. The glossy finish over the design comes from the glass plate itself. Finally, Rosemary seals the wrong side of the collage with a few coats of varnish to protect the work. The finished piece is strictly for decorative use.

"Anytime I travel I look for papers to use in my designs," says Rosemary. As the result of her searches, she has a library of brochures, cards, and other decorative paper scraps destined to be a part of her decoupage under glass. ❧

Above: This tuneful group has been getting together for about 20 years to call friends and family around the country and sing their greetings over the telephone. Everyone gathers around the table (painted by hostess Linda McIntosh, in the purple blouse) and takes turns calling out numbers to be dialed. (Inset): The daylong party has always included an exchange of handmade gifts as well.

28

A Ringing, Singing Christmas Card

*I*t's a chilly, gray day in Modoc, South Carolina, but inside the home of Linda McIntosh and Helen Hendee, there's a warm fire and tables are spread with food. About a dozen women sit around a table in front of the fireplace.

Patty May, the designated dialer, punches in the first telephone number, holds up the receiver, and everyone bursts into an enthusiastic rendition of "We Wish You a Merry Christmas." Patty closes by saying, "Merry Christmas from Santa and his elves," and rings off. This routine is repeated all afternoon (interrupted by frequent laughter and joking) as the group works its way through each person's address book.

The recipients of these calls are family, friends, clients, and co-workers of the women assembled, as well as their dentists, doctors, and even a veterinarian (whose greeting is sung in "woofs"). Most of these people are in Augusta, Georgia, only 30 minutes away, but calls also go to people across the country and even around the world.

The party is always on a weekday—that makes it easier to locate the people to be called—and the women take a vacation day from work, if necessary, to make sure they can attend. Later, when the telephone bill comes in, it circulates among the friends, and each pays for the calls made on her behalf.

"It started informally," Linda says of the gathering. A group of special education teachers from Gracewood State School got together and began calling friends they didn't see often and caroling to them. Then the gathering grew and became a party that lasted most of the day. "Now it's something we look forward to every year," says Linda. "You get to spread around the cheer with a lot of people, and it gets you in the holiday spirit." The recipients of the calls look forward to it, too. "If we miss someone, we hear about it," she adds. More than one person on the receiving end exclaims, "Thank you! You all make my Christmas every year!" ❦

Above: Linda McIntosh and Helen Hendee decorate their lake house inside and out for the party. Even the goose decoy gets dressed up for the season with a wreath and bow.

Above: Handcrafted ornaments exchanged over the years include twig stars, starfish Santas, painted eggs, and whimsical Christmas puppies made from dog biscuits.

The Romance Of Linen and Lace

Anne Adams of Keatchie, Louisiana, began collecting old laces and linens when she was a partner in an antiques shop. "There's just something about the old laces that you don't get in the new ones—a romance," she says.

Anne uses her collection to make Christmas decorations and accessories for her own home and for sale. Every year she holds an open house, an event she calls the Christmas Cottage.

The handkerchief angels are one of her most popular creations. A fabric version of the traditional English "cracker" also sells well, because it does double duty as a decorative accessory and a gift container for small surprises. Instead of popping open like paper ones, it unties at each end.

For Anne, collecting laces and linens is its own reward. Being able to turn them into Christmas treasures for her own and others' enjoyment makes the reward that much sweeter.

MAKE YOUR OWN VICTORIAN TREASURES

To clean and whiten the linens and laces she finds at estate sales and flea markets, Anne dissolves Purex and Biz detergent in water, then pours the two solutions into a large jar full of warm water. She adds the textiles and shakes the jar gently. "That's better than scrubbing them," she says, "because scrubbing can break the fibers." She then rinses them at least 10 times. It's essential to get out all of the soap; otherwise the linen will scorch when you press it.

To make the angels for her tree, Anne soaks a clean linen handkerchief in undiluted liquid starch; then she squeezes out the excess starch and spreads the handkerchief to dry. While it's still slightly damp, she irons the cloth. Then she drapes the handkerchief over a small craft foam ball, ties it with ribbon, and adds Spanish moss for hair. (For details, see "Christmas Workroom," which begins on page 140.)

To make the crackers, Anne covers cardboard tubes with fabric, handstitches lace to the ends, and ties each end with ribbon. ❧

Above: Inspired by the gift tag in the foreground, Anne created linen-and-lace English "crackers" to sell at her annual Christmas Cottage open house.

Top: Anne Adams turns antique handkerchiefs into angels for her tree. Each handkerchief is different—the one she's holding features drawn threadwork, while others are trimmed with lace or crocheted edgings.

Above: One-of-a-kind stockings and angels, fashioned from beautiful old laces, are collectibles themselves. The angels are dolls or tree-toppers that Anne drapes with strips of lace and doilies. Fabric, a doily, or more lace makes the wings.

Picture-Perfect Package Wraps

Presents of every shape and size, piled under the tree, are a celebration of the Christmas season. Often, the wrap on each gift reveals the identity of the giver—Grandmother lovingly bundles hand-knitted sweaters in tissue-thin wrapping paper, and a dear friend tops each package with a handmade ornament.

Dondra Parham, assistant editor for this book, treasures her mother's signature gift wrappings, pictured here. It's not difficult to do—you need only a card saved from last season and a piece of foil-backed wrapping paper, along with your usual wrapping supplies.

Cut along the fold of an old Christmas card. From the card back, trim ⅛ inch off all edges. From the foil-backed gift wrap, cut a piece that is 1 inch larger all around than the card front. Using a glue stick, glue the card front on the package top. Center and stack the card back and the foil-backed paper, shiny side down, on top of the card

front. Glue the outer edges of the foil-backed paper to the package top, well outside the card front. Using complementary paper, wrap the box.

With your fingertips, find the edges of the card front through the layers of gift wrap. Draw the back of your thumbnail along these edges to crease the paper, marking the position of the card front. Place a ruler on the diagonal between two corners of the outline. Using a craft knife, cut through the outer wrapping paper and the foil-backed paper along the straight edge. Reposition the ruler between the remaining corners, and then cut through the papers again. (The card back will protect the card front from an accidental cut.) Open the flaps, and remove the card back. Then, treating both layers of paper as one, roll back the paper flaps to frame the card front. Where the illustration on the card allows, you can write a personalized note directly on the package instead of adding a gift tag. ❦

Special Stockings For Bundles of Joy

The stork may bring babies the rest of the year, but in December it's Santa's job—at least, that's how it seems at St. Vincent's Hospital in Birmingham, Alabama. Babies born the week before Christmas leave the hospital with—or sometimes in—a large, bright red stocking like the kind Santa fills.

The Pink Ladies of St. Vincent's Hospital have been making stockings for Christmas babies since 1964. Zuma Brentnal, manager of volunteer services at the hospital, saw the idea in a nursing journal, but the stockings pictured were just plain fabric. She and longtime volunteer Hilda Baker knew they could do something more creative. They designed stockings of red cotton outing with white cuffs, felt figures, and sequin trims; the members of the auxiliary stitched them by hand. Each stocking takes about eight to 10 hours to make, and no two are alike.

Hilda starts buying fabric January 1. "It takes four people to buy the fabric," she says, "because we have to get so much." She also shops for sequins and trims at after-Christmas sales. Over the next several months, she cuts out the boots, cuffs, and felt figures and packages them into kits. Then members of the auxiliary take them home to assemble. "Some women love to do it," says Hilda. "One lady made 85 this year. Some only do one." By the week before Christmas, however, the group will have made more than 100 stockings. Inside each one is a label that reads "Made especially for you by the Pink Ladies of St. Vincent's Hospital." ❧

Top right: The Pink Ladies have been sending newborns home with their very own Christmas stockings since 1964.

Bottom right: Volunteers (left to right) Hilda Baker, Gen Pharo, and Katherine Stephens appliqué stockings for babies born at St. Vincent's Hospital just before Christmas.

These Centerpieces Hide a Surprise

Above: Baltimore flower designer Elizabeth Nuttle maintains a childhood tradition: Ribbons lead from each place setting to a gift hidden under the mound of "snow."

When Elizabeth Nuttle of Baltimore, Maryland, was a child, some of Santa's surprises were distributed in a special way. On the dining table was a snowy mountain of cotton batting, with Santa in a sleigh perched on top. Ribbons led from each place setting to the cottony mound, and after dinner, everyone pulled carefully on his or her ribbon to draw out a small gift hidden under the "snow."

The tradition began with her great-grandmother, and Elizabeth's mother continued it. Now Elizabeth keeps up the custom and shares it with the friends who join her to celebrate the holidays.

Her sleigh, Santa, and reindeer are the same ones her great-grandmother used. To adapt the idea for your family's table, use a Santa or any collection of figures you happen to have—angels, carolers, or a little village of houses. First, stack boxes or books or turn bowls upside down to position the figures at the desired heights. Next, group small wrapped packages around this base so that each person's gift will be close to his place at the table. Tape a piece of ribbon to each package, making sure the ribbon is long enough to reach the corresponding place setting. Finally, cover the base and gifts with batting and nestle the figures into the snow.

Margie Deitz of Fitz & Floyd suggests a variation on this idea for holiday luncheons with friends. Let the gifts themselves be the centerpiece—spread them on the table and then tie one end of a piece of ribbon around a package and the other end around the napkin at the recipient's place setting. Use a small topiary tree or a soft-sculpture Santa to anchor the centerpiece visually. You may want to wrap extra boxes to place around the tree or Santa for a full, festive look even after the gifts have been claimed.

To make the tree, glue sheet moss to a craft foam cone, then wrap it with wired star garland and strands of beads. Fern pins (also called greening pins or pole pins) will hold the beads in place. Top the tree with an angel or a star for a tablescape that celebrates the gift-giving season. 🍂

Above: The type of wrapping paper and ribbon you choose will set the mood. Wine-colored satin ribbon, green grosgrain, and an assortment of red, green, and gold-print papers give this centerpiece a rich, warm look. Silver and gold papers and opalescent ribbon would be glitzy and elegant, while curling ribbons and brightly colored papers would set the stage for a children's holiday party.

Above: Reaching the island is almost as much fun as the party itself. The dock where guests arrive by boat is nearly hidden by the natural growth. The waters near the dock are a safe haven for the endangered manatee.

A Progressive Party
In Paradise

Tucked away along the southwestern Gulf Coast of Florida lies a skinny barrier island no longer than seven miles and no wider than one-half mile. There are no paved roads and no automobiles, only golf carts, and the only way to or from the island is by boat. Along the Gulf side of the island, a blanket of shells covers the pristine beach, while on the bay side, calmer waters provide an ideal place for the boat docks and a home for the endangered manatee.

Throughout the year, the island serves primarily as a haven for mainlanders who want to escape from harried city life. Even at Christmas, it offers a special kind of refuge to the members of the local homeowners' association. For the last 13 years, they've been hosting a "progressive party" for family and friends on this isle of paradise.

"The idea started when someone invited the neighborhood for hors d'oeuvres," recalls Bette Dewey. "Then someone else decided that dinner

Above: Competition is fierce on the island when it comes to decorating the golf carts. Here, one cart sports a stocking on its front grill, another wears a crown of small Christmas lights, and a third is wreathed with holly.

Above: Florida's mild temperatures permit shorts and bare feet at this Christmas party. On the Deweys' wraparound deck, guests can enjoy a view of the ocean while they eat dinner.

should be at their house. Later, we added a bonfire for the children and grandchildren. Because we start so early, we can spend a good deal of time at each place, and one person doesn't end up doing all the work."

Arriving for the festivities is almost as much fun as the party itself. Boatloads of guests are shuttled to the dock and then whisked away in golf carts decorated by competitive neighbors. Because the temperature ranges from a mild 75° to 80° during December, the dress is very casual, with guests decked out in shorts and Hawaiian shirts.

The party begins with cocktails and light hors d'oeuvres, usually at Judy and Don Meline's home, which is only minutes from the dock. Afterward, the guests move on to dinner, with most choosing to walk the short distance to the next house. Hosted by Bette and Wayne Dewey, the sumptuous feast features a variety of mouthwatering dishes brought by guests.

Dinner is planned so that most people finish eating just as the sun begins to set. For a grand finale, the party makes its way to the beach. Everyone settles down on towels tossed around a roaring bonfire to watch a spectacular sunset across the Gulf. 🌿

Opposite: Everyone contributes something to the dinner buffet at Bette and Wayne Dewey's home. To make the table festive, Bette draped it with silver lamé, bunched and gathered to frame the array of food. Pillar candles were wrapped with silver mesh layered over pink metallic ribbon. Garnishes of fruit, hibiscus, greenery, and berries add bright finishing touches that make each dish even more appealing.

Above: After dinner, the party reconvenes around a bonfire at the beach to watch the sun set.

39

Decorating
for the Holidays

Reminders echo one another in this mountain retreat. To lift the eye and emphasize a feeling of spaciousness, Hal Ainsworth and Winton Noah take the decorations all the way to the ceiling. A collection of antique French gypsy carousel puppets line the mantel. Pheasant feathers, decorative birds, and a pair of wax horns enliven the greenery overhead.

Deck the Halls With Feathers and Fir

Whimsical might not be the first word that springs to mind when you visit the showroom of Hal Ainsworth and Winton Noah at the Atlanta Decorative Arts Center. The things they buy on frequent trips to Europe are usually opulent and elegant. But there's a sense of whimsy, too, and it's even more readily apparent in their Highlands, North Carolina, weekend retreat.

Here, white pine interiors provide a rustic setting for locally made twig furniture. "It's not serious and that's its charm," Hal says of the folk-art furniture. And it suits the setting, he adds. "It's like bringing the woods indoors." Combining these pieces with oriental carpets, plaid upholstery, and antiques from the south of France yields an eminently civilized home away from home.

"We love it up here," says Winton. "We come up here about 40 weekends out of the year." At Christmastime, it has become their tradition to host a party for employees, clients, and local friends on the weekend of the Highlands Christmas parade.

Above: Each December Hal (in the doorway) and Winton (on the step) invite about 60 clients, friends, and employees to join them in Highlands, North Carolina, to watch the town's Christmas parade and then gather for a late lunch.

Above: Antique brass-mounted horns stand on top of the English apothecary shelf and serve as vases for sprays of pheasant feathers. Bamboo skewers join apples and oranges; greenery, pinecones, horns, and feathers are wedged or wired in place.

From the road below, you can barely see the roof and chimney of the house—it is completely hidden by the dense growth of wild rhododendrons. The original structure was built in 1957, and Hal and Winton enlarged it by building over and around it. They raised the ceilings to 15 feet at the peak and added living and dining areas, a kitchen, sitting room, and deck (recently enclosed to make a screened porch). When the new house was finished, the little house inside was taken apart and removed.

At Christmas, Hal and Winton decorate the house with fruit, Fraser fir, pheasant feathers, pinecones, and poinsettias. They use these simple materials lavishly and dress up every major focal point. "In the showroom, we live with clutter—what we call 'organized clutter,'" says Hal. "And if you're that sort of person, seeing a bald spot drives you crazy." There are no bald spots here.

Antique hunting trophies and sporting equipment fill the walls and lift the eye toward the high ceiling. The Christmas decorations do the same: They're massed on top of the breakfront, the apothecary shelf, and a tall bookcase, as well as above the doors. Even a high shelf holding large crocks receives a bit of greenery. Because the

Opposite: Plaid fabric and oriental carpets give the house a Christmassy feeling all year. On the table, a teddy bear occupies a toy regimental guardhouse, and red candles add a seasonal note.

44

Above: A birch-and-black-walnut breakfront made by a Highlands, North Carolina, craftsman fills one wall in the sitting area. It is crowned with greenery, fruit, honeysuckle-vine reindeer, and items that evoke the spirit of a childhood Christmas: a stuffed bear, a birdhouse, an antique French regimental drum, and an old bird cage. On the sconce hangs a fresh fir wreath with a bouquet of pheasant feathers.

46

Above: Twenty-one strings of tiny bulbs outline this fir tree's branches with twinkling light. Tissue paper, loosely crumpled and stuffed around the base of the tree, hides the stand. The painted twig furniture is crafted locally, using rhododendron trunks and branches.

rooms in the house flow freely into one another, the same materials are used throughout to create a unified look.

The smells of Christmas are here, too. Bowls of apples distributed through the house fill the air with fruity fragrance. Scraps of fir from the Christmas tree are tossed into the fire, releasing a wonderful aroma as they burn.

Winton comes from a big family in Denton, Texas. "Everyone got together on Christmas Eve and Christmas Day at my grandmother's house," he recalls. "There were lots of pies, turkey, dressing, fresh vegetables—my relatives were all good cooks and they all liked to eat." Winton carries on that tradition at the North Carolina Christmas lunch by making sure the menu is bountiful. Hal grew up in Hazelhurst, Mississippi, where his grandmother often held parties for the family and neighbors. Her flair for creating festive occasions on the spur of the moment clearly lives on in

Above: An assortment of favorite things becomes a festive focal point with the addition of a basket of bright red poinsettias, a bowl of apples, and a red candle. An antique box filled with pheasant-feather balls and fir echoes the Christmas decorations throughout the house.

47

Hal. The Christmas decorations that set a holiday mood are chiefly his handiwork. And with the help of an employee from the Atlanta office, he sets up the bar and lays out the buffet so that everything is as attractive as it is tasty.

For Hal and Winton, entertaining taps another side of the creativity that fuels their professional lives. At the Highlands gathering, good food and good wine in a well-decorated setting make for a memorable holiday celebration. 🐦

TIPS FOR HOLIDAY ENTERTAINING

A buffet is the easiest way to serve large numbers of people. If you set up the table so that guests can pick up a plate and silverware at either end, you'll minimize long, cafeteria-style lines. Placing the drinks elsewhere also helps reduce crowding around the food table.

Hal believes that food is all the more appetizing when it's beautifully presented, so he garnishes everything liberally. Leaf lettuce, which he buys by the box from the grocer, makes frilly green frames for the roast pig, the turkey, and the asparagus. Oranges, apples, lemon slices, and cherry tomatoes add bright color.

Above: The house is small, so Hal and Winton put one bar on the porch and another on the deck to spread out the crowd.

Right: For a colorful presentation, Hal places asparagus in a dish and spreads baby carrots in a band across the middle.

Below right: With a bow for a bustle, the turkey looks almost too fancy to eat—but it's not. Hal ties the turkey legs together with a ribbon and tucks the bow into the cavity. When it's time to carve the turkey, he just snips the ribbon away.

Above: The buffet table is set up so that guests can start at either end and circle around. A whole roast pig fills the center of the table. Sliced tenderloin and turkey are placed at the ends, along with bread, condiments, and vegetables.

Above: Turn a standard honeysuckle-vine wreath into a Christmas classic by hot-gluing twiggy branches and artificial lemons and leaves to it. For more on where to find lemons like these, see Resources, page 156.

Lemons and Leaves
On a Honeysuckle Vine

Here's a simple way to give an old vine wreath a fresh, new look. Floral designer Joe Smith of Nashville, Tennessee, added artificial lemons, branches, birds' nests, and elegant wire-edge ribbon to a ring of honeysuckle vine for a wreath that combines classic good looks with today's taste for naturals.

To make it, start with a vine wreath 19 inches in diameter. Using a hot-glue gun, coat the ends of twiggy branches, such as huckleberry, with glue and work them into the woven vines. This gives the wreath more dimension and a freer line.

Next, add lemons in groups of two or three around the wreath and frame each group with clusters of leaves. Be sure to bend and curl the leaves to suggest a more natural effect. Glue small pads of moss between the bunches of lemons and among the leaves for accents of soft texture and bright green color.

Wire purchased birds' nests to the vine wreath and use hot glue to hold them in the desired position. Nestle purchased paper eggs in the nests or make your own eggs by covering craft foam eggs with tissue paper and sponging them with thinned acrylic paint.

To finish, make a shoestring bow from the wire-edge ribbon, pinching the loops at the middle and securing with florist's wire. Wire the bow to the wreath, then crimp and curl the streamers, tucking them among the leaves for a more active line. ❦

Beyond the Big Red Bow

Used everywhere from the mailbox to the mantel, a big Christmas bow is a decorating tradition. The sentimental favorite is red velvet, but one visit to the craft or fabric store reveals a whole world of decorative ribbons.

"Because of the profusion of ribbon available now, both in quantity and quality, your selection of ribbon has become almost a statement by itself," notes Dorothy McDaniel, a floral designer in Homewood, Alabama.

The Christmas palette has expanded to include amethyst and other jewel tones, along with time-honored red and green. (Gold, followed by silver and copper, is always strong for the holidays.) The real ribbon renaissance, however, is due to the fact that the materials from which ribbons are made have expanded right along with the choice of color. Woven ribbons now have wire edges. Lustrous metal mesh ribbons are gaining in popularity. Even paper has taken a glamorous twist!

Dorothy chooses wire-edge ribbon bows for many of her wreaths and badges. "You get the illusion of more movement with the wired ribbons," she says. "It is pricier, but it takes less ribbon to make an important bow because you can shape the loops and they hold their form."

When decorating outdoors, choose ribbon that is waterproof and colorfast. One of the most popular of such ribbons is Veltex®, a flocked ribbon from Berwick, the nation's largest manufacturer of ribbons and bows. (The company produces three million bows a day.) According to national sales manager Larry Stoffer, red is still the favorite color for this ribbon.

Donna Horack, an Atlanta member of the American Society of Interior Designers, believes that bows can be made even bigger and better by combining red velvet, for example, with other types of ribbons. "Using a variety of textures in one bow adds depth to your design. And it's exciting, giving your eye something more to look at than just red or gold," she adds. Donna shared with us her secret to making a better big red bow (opposite).

To store bows until next season, Donna advises that you fasten one bow on each end of a coat hanger. Then cover the pair with a lightweight plastic dry cleaning bag to keep off dust and place the coat hanger in your attic or closet. ❧

Above: Give a new twist to customary Christmas decorations with updated ribbons. Smart styles include vivid jewel tones and chic patterns, as seen in this explosion of ribbons from Berwick Industries, Inc., in Marietta, Georgia.

HOW TO MAKE A DESIGNER BOW

Donna stacks three bows of graduated diameters to make this show-stopping decoration. She recommends doubling the florist's wire to ensure a strong tie. For a large bow, from wire, cut 1 (36") length; fold wire in half and twist ends together. For a small bow, cut 1 (18") length of wire; fold and twist ends together.

Materials:
florist's wire
4½ yards (2½"-wide) red velvet ribbon
3½ yards (2½"-wide) gold wire-edge ribbon
4 yards (2"-wide) plaid ribbon

1. To begin, make a 12"-diameter red velvet bow. Measure 6" from ribbon end and pinch the ribbon between your forefinger and thumb. This point is the center of the bow. Make a 6" loop and pinch the ribbon again at the bow center. Then twist ribbon one half turn and make second loop on opposite side.

2. Make five loops on either side of the center in the same manner. Continue to hold the bow at the center between your forefinger and thumb. When working with wide, heavy ribbon, such as the red velvet, you may have to use your whole hand to manage the bow. Fold the doubled florist's wire over the center of the bow.

3. Fold the bow in half across the wire. Hold the bow firmly in one hand. Using the other hand, tightly twist the ends of the florist's wire together. If necessary, use needle-nose pliers to tighten the wire.

4. Fluff the bow by pulling firmly on the loops. Because the wire is securely fastened around the center, the loops cannot be pulled out of shape.

5. From gold ribbon, make a 10"-diameter bow in the same manner. To nest the gold bow into the red, wrap the wires from the gold bow over the

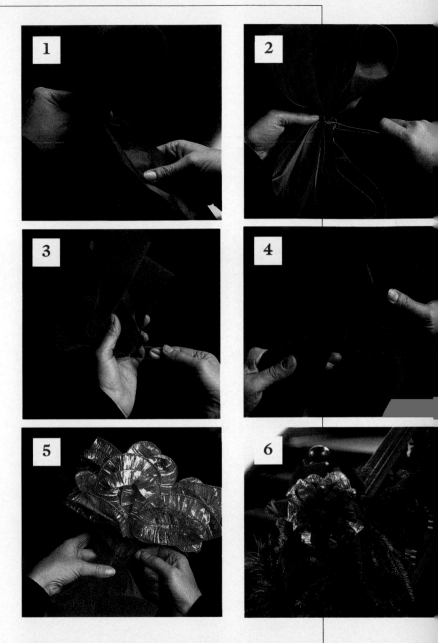

center of the red bow. Twist ends of all wires together behind the red bow.

6. From plaid ribbon, make an 8"-diameter bow and nest it in the center of the gold-and-red bow in the same manner. To make streamers, fold remaining length of plaid ribbon in half. Tuck streamers behind the gold bow, allowing the ends to hang freely.

Historic Savannah: Decorating Downtown

The mere mention of Savannah, Georgia, conjures up images of gentility and hospitality, both legendary Southern attributes. Speak of Savannah at Christmastime and you add the rich visual pleasures of the season to an already romanticized city.

The downtown's curbside appeal has developed from the master plan of James Oglethorpe, who, in 1733, founded the British settlement on a sandy river bluff 18 miles inland from the Atlantic coast. His urban plan called for an orderly arrangement of squares, or common areas, which continue to give definition to the surrounding neighborhoods. Today the National Historic Landmark District not only preserves the architecture and the city plan, but also fosters a sense of community among its residents.

In December the Savannah Hospitality Foundation and Historic Savannah Foundation, Inc., sponsor a holiday doorway contest. Leslie Langford, who helps chair the contest, says competition is keen in both business and residential classes for the upscale prizes. "When one participant noticed our judges at his door, he raced to replace a light bulb," she reports. "It's great fun to know we all do our best to look good through the holidays." On these pages, we bring you a sampling of Savannah's most savvy doorway themes.

The Downing residence (opposite and right) epitomizes the elegance of Savannah at Christmastime. The three-story town house rises straight from the sidewalk. Living ivy topiaries are linked by an elaborate magnolia garland, eloquently interpreting the grandeur of this structure.

Opposite: Magnolia leaves form a regal garland over the Italianate pediment of this 19th-century town house. A spiral of lights wraps both the garland and the topiaries. Bunching several strands of miniature lights achieves a formal and impressive presentation.

Above: A stroll around Chippewa Square takes you past the Downing residence. The conical ivy topiaries that flank the entry are planted in sphagnum moss supported by a PVC frame. Moss-covered dove finials with outstretched wings carry tulip bouquets.

Above: Approaching decorating with an artist's eye, Ann Osteen pulled together this vivid doorway treatment from mementos of her trip to China. The energetic combination of Eastern color and Western glitter catches attention from blocks away.

Across the district, Abby Buckwald's home (opposite) faces Whitefield Square. "I have a little place in the country, so this was supposed to be my 'serious city house,'" she confesses. Abby's whimsical decorating style, however, overtook her aspirations to urbane splendor. "Now I have two country houses—this one just happens to be in the city." For the holidays she outfits the porch with an ivy swag, while the windows sport crescents of ivy topped with a punch-ribbon bow.

Along the riverfront, refurbished buildings contain specialty shops, eateries, and inns. Ann Osteen's home and gallery (above) is in such a structure on Factor's Walk. Influenced by travels to China, she adopted an East-meets-West motif for her traffic-stopping decorations.

Ann simply draped star garland around a Chinese paper kite. Then she hung the kite from the door knocker, along with a flashy souvenir banner from China's New Year celebration. On

Above: Abby Buckwald's home has all the charms of a country house despite the downtown address. Ivy cuttings festoon the door, trailing into the two ficus trees, which are year-round front porch fixtures. Twinkling lights and dried hydrangea tucked into the ivy add to the casual spirit.

the shutters to either side of the door, she placed more of the Chinese keepsakes, accented by a coil of metallic twist ribbon. "When I bought that gold twist, the girl at the checkout said that she had to use a vise and have her husband's help to untwist the stuff," Ann recalls. "I told her that I wasn't going to untwist it—I was going to use it just like that."

Adjacent to historic Savannah is the city's Victorian district, where Betty Hendrix Nease has returned her home to its former glory (left). "It took 54 quarts of paint, each one shade apart, to get seven perfect colors on my house," says Betty.

For her home's Christmas finery, Betty enlisted the help of floral designer Joanne Nelson. "I knew Betty wanted to use greenery and fruit—things that would have been available in the 1800s," says Joanne. "I also knew there had to be a lot of it, because that suited the house."

Betty spent hours stringing fresh cranberries onto florist's wire to dress the entry, banisters, and door and window badges to the designer's specifications. "I kept asking Joanne if I really had to string all those berries, and she said that I did," laughs Betty. To her delight, contest judges awarded Betty the grand prize for her effort.

Residents of downtown Savannah heartily celebrate the rich and diverse architectural heritage of the city's landmark districts. While that spirit transcends the seasons, it is especially heightened at Christmastime, when a little friendly competition inspires neighbors to enhance the historic buildings with garlands and wreaths, ribbons and lights—delighting both the eye and the heart. 🍎

Top left: Gilded pineapples beaded with jewel-like cranberries become fanciful newel post ornaments. To secure the berries, use U-shaped wires or hairpins. "I tried using straight wires at first, and the berries just slid off," says floral designer Joanne Nelson. (For instructions on making this Victorian-inspired decoration, see "Christmas Workroom," which begins on page 140.)

Bottom left: The elaborate arrangements of this circa 1871 home recall the decorative whims of the Victorian era. Cranberries strung on florist's wire are used throughout as an accent garland.

Tree and Stair Are A Matchless Pair

Placing the Christmas tree in the curve of the stairwell increases the impact of both tree and staircase. At Evelynton, in historic Charles City, Virginia, the architecture frames the tree, creating a spectacular welcome for guests coming into the wide entrance hall.

The 55-foot-long garland on the stair rail is made from cuttings of Leyland cypress that are attached to a length of clothesline with reel wire. (See "Christmas Workroom," beginning on page 140, for more information about making a garland.) To protect the wood from scratches, the roping is secured to the stair rail with green pipe cleaners.

At the bottom of the stairs, where the banister curls like a nautilus shell around the newel post, floral designer Annie Black rests an arrangement of Leyland cypress and fruit. "The container fits the space perfectly," she explains, "and it holds about six blocks of Oasis. When that's wet, it's heavy enough to keep the arrangement from tipping over." An ornamental pineapple and red and green apples on florist's picks crown the branches. Annie lightly gilded the apples with Rub 'n Buff®. "It enhances the fruit and makes it richer," she says. Big bows and long streamers of copper and brocade ribbons complete the arrangement.

Copper ribbon also festoons the stair rail and the tree, linking them visually. Artificial fruit sprayed gold hangs from the branches, and gold tassels and wreaths made from drapery cord decorate the tree for a lavish effect.

Originally part of Westover plantation, home of William Byrd II, Evelynton has been in the Ruffin family for about 200 years. The house is currently used for weddings, receptions, and corporate entertaining. ❦

Right: Copper ribbon and gilded fruit provide the decorating theme in the entrance hall of Evelynton in Virginia. The Georgian-style house was built in 1937, replacing a structure that burned during the Civil War.

Above: Tans, creams, and golds dress this mantel with the color of candlelight. Dried hydrangea pinned to a straw base forms the wreath. Gold drapery tiebacks embellish both the wreath and the angels below.

Make the Most of the Mantel

You can give an entire room a festive feeling simply by decorating the fireplace. To make the most of the opportunity, be sure to decorate both the chimney breast and the mantel shelf.

The mantel above is appealingly understated. To make the wreath, collect oakleaf hydrangea flowers that have dried on the bush. Be sure to gather the flowers before they become too brittle, or they'll shatter as you try to work with them. Pin the flowers to a straw wreath form, using U-shaped fern pins. Add small bunches of miniature baby's breath for ivory highlights. Pin gold drapery tiebacks to the wreath for an elegant flourish.

You can also duplicate the angels flanking the wreath. They were inexpensive plastic figures that owner Marilyn Michael "aged" with a wash of burnt sienna acrylic paint. Then she lightly brushed them with gold, letting the colors in the folds and creases show through.

An elaborate chimney breast like the one at Evelynton, in Virginia (opposite), is a good candidate for a garland outline. Its Georgian-style molding and fluted pilasters frame a portrait of the

Opposite: A boxwood-and-fir garland wrapped with gold cord frames a drawing room mantel. On the mantel shelf, potted amaryllis, narcissus, and ivy suggest a Christmas garden blooming amid a bed of evergreen boughs.

58

house's current owner, Edmund S. Ruffin, at age 15. The garland of boxwood, noble fir, and dried myrtle berries, hung from tiny nails in the woodwork, emphasizes the effect. The swag falls just over the top of the picture frame.

To make the badges at the corners, floral designer Annie Black wired together branches of noble fir. Then, instead of wiring the fruit into the badges, she used a hot-glue gun. "As soon as you pierce the fruit with wire, it starts to decay," she says, "and the decorations at Evelynton have to stay up all month." She used both low-melt and standard hot glue and says that the heat of the glue did not appear to "cook" the fruit or shorten its life in the arrangement.

On the mantel shelf, pots of forced narcissus and amaryllis flank the portrait, and potted ivy cascades over the mantel at the center. Hemlock branches hide the pots, so the flowers seem to bloom from a blanket of green.

If you plan to force amaryllis or narcissus yourself, you'll need to start the bulbs about four to six weeks before you need them in bloom. Or you can buy flowering plants in December from a nursery or a florist.

Paper and wire stars and a bright plaid bow make the fresh wreath at left festive. Positioning the stars at different angles yields a more interesting effect than would simply placing them flat against the wreath. On the mantel below, a pair of gilded papier-mâché deer flank the wreath, and Italian cherubs hold paper stars against the mantel lamps.

For more on these stars and Evelynton's garlands and badges, see "Christmas Workroom," starting on page 140. 🐦

Top left: An Italian angel, wired to the mantel lamp, holds a painted-and-collaged star in place. Artist and interior designer Linda McIntosh made the stars for the Augusta, Georgia, Festival of Trees.

Bottom left: This evergreen wreath twinkles with two kinds of stars—solid ones, made from watercolor paper marbleized with metallic paints, and star silhouettes, formed from gold paper-covered wire.

Clove-Studded Stars

Our Texas-sized craft foam stars are 9 inches, 6 inches, and 3½ inches across. Buy precut pieces or cut your own from ½- to 1-inch-thick craft foam. For each star, seal the craft foam by applying a coat of gesso and let dry. Next, paint the star with yellow acrylic paint and let dry.

To add texture, apply acrylic matte sealer to one surface of the painted star. While still wet, lightly sprinkle the surface with terra-cotta-colored craft sand; the sand will adhere to the sealer. Working on one surface at a time, repeat to add texture to the entire star. Begin by dusting the star with just a light layer of sand, adding more sand in a second layer of sealer if a deeper orange color is desired. When dry, gently apply a thin topcoat of sealer over the sand.

Push clove stems into the textured stars to make spirals, starbursts, and other traditional pomander patterns. To hang as a Christmas tree ornament, use a large-eyed needle to thread a 10-inch length of ⅛-inch-wide gold ribbon through a point of the star. Knot ribbon ends to form a loop. ❧

Above: For a Southwest spin on a Christmas memory, craft these clove-studded stars. Yellow paint overlaid with terra-cotta-colored sand creates the illusion of an orange-peel surface.

Quick Ideas for Coffee Tables

Atlanta interior designer Charles Gandy, a Fellow of the American Society of Interior Designers, devised these easy-to-assemble centerpieces following his own philosophy of decorating: Simplify, then exaggerate. "I may reduce a scheme to two or three elements," he says, "and then use hundreds of them."

This approach works, he says, because he balances unity with diversity. For example, he uses one color of ribbon in several different textures or lots of candles in one color but of different sizes. And, he adds, "Don't be timid." You can achieve a lavish effect with inexpensive florist's ribbon simply by using yards of it. For the spontaneous quality of the decorations shown here, Charles lets the ribbon curl and fall naturally. To make rings of votive candle holders easier to assemble, use a platter or plate as a guide.

For the table below, alternate votive candles and red satin balls in a ring. Weave red florist's ribbon and wired star garland through the arrangement to lead the eye around the circle. (Keep both materials away from the flames.) Scatter jingle bells in the center to add sparkle.

Above: Make a ring of votive candles and large red Christmas tree balls and weave ribbon and star garland around the circle. Scatter jingle bells in the center.

To reproduce the twinkling tabletop at right, place glass custard cups and clear votive candle holders upside down in a utility pan and wind red florist's ribbon around them. Fill the pan with water and place tin stars on the glass pedestals. Float votive candles among the stars. (For a mail order source of tin stars, see Resources, page 156.)

To make the "wreath" on the right below, fill clear votive candle holders with water and add a few drops of green food coloring to each. Space votive candles evenly around the outside to give the wreath depth. Suggest a bow and streamers with randomly placed red ribbons. Jingle bells and wired star garland add whimsy and color.

For a last-minute centerpiece, collect all of your candlesticks and votive candle holders and group them in the middle of the table (below). Wind three or four kinds of red ribbon among them—Charles used punch ribbon, florist's ribbon, and narrow satin ribbon, along with wired star garland. All of these materials will burn or melt, so be sure to keep them well away from the flames. ❧

Above: Rest tin stars on glass containers in a water-filled pan and float votives among them.

Above: Group all of your candles in the center of the table and embellish with lots of ribbon.

Above: Fill votive candle holders with water and tint with green food coloring.

Above: White tapers in crystal and silver candlesticks cast a romantic glow over dinner. The grouping has at its base a mirrored runner that unites the individual elements—candles, gifts, and antique boxes. Flanking the centerpiece, Austrian brandy snifters hold airy bouquets of alstroemeria, Ming fern, baby's breath, and garden ivy.

64

Put Your Collection in the Center

*E*legance that can be achieved easily is especially desirable during the holiday season. With a few tips from successful hosts and designers, followed by a tour through your own collectibles, you'll be prepared to create a tablescape as inviting as any of these.

Color and theme unify the elements in the romantic setting shown here, by Andrea Hubbard, a member of the American Society of Interior Designers. "To hold the design together, each of the package wraps features a bit of glitz in the same silver and white tones of the candlesticks," she explains. Andrea pressed into table service an unconventional collection: The antique sterling boxes found among the packages are ladies' compacts that belong to the homeowner.

Above: Exquisitely wrapped gift boxes are the heart of this table setting. Gold, silver, and white wrappings link the packages with the sparkling tones of the various candlesticks. A variety of ribbons, including gold and silver mesh and iridescent net, tie up the packages, adding texture, sparkle, and interest. Beads and baubles top the bows and lace through the other decorative elements.

Rosemary for remembrance and mounds of fruit for color create a bountiful centerpiece at Sally Berry's home in Sandy Springs, Georgia (opposite). Sally insists that decorating be simple, especially when Christmas dinner brings more than two dozen guests to her table. "When the family gathering is at your house, you have two primary responsibilities," she explains. "You've got to decorate and you've got to find everybody a place to sit!"

Dan Snyder of Savannah, Georgia, makes this suggestion as a guide in setting a holiday table: "Use items with strong color or interest, and then balance these with neutral pieces." On his table (right), white Wedgwood and ecru linen are perfect counterparts to the combination of Bavarian cut glass, Victorian cranberry glass, and Imari ware soup bowls at each place.

Serious collections of silver and glass, multiples of commonplace porcelain pieces, or a crafty grouping of topiaries and pomanders are treasures that can be almost effortlessly assembled to decorate your holiday table. ❦

Top right: By invitation, Santa parachutes into this well-ordered interior. Unexpected, frivolous elements—such as the suspended ornament and the kitschy snow globe—add a note of humor to this otherwise sophisticated setting.

Bottom right: Blue-and-white porcelain bowls filled with easy-to-find ornaments form the foundation of this minimalist approach to a holiday setting. The eclectically assembled glassware and china reflect the host's preference for—and confidence in—mixing patterns at each place.

Opposite: Dressed with French silk ribbon, these herb-covered topiaries stand on a tapestry runner. Tucked in among the apples, pears, cranberries, and nuts are bales and globes of aromatic dried materials. To make the topiaries or the bales, see "Christmas Workroom," beginning on page 140.

Christmas Treasures

These Decorations Are Naturally Elegant

Southerners love to bring foliage in from the garden to decorate their homes for the holidays. Here are four ornaments that will bring some natural loveliness indoors.

Our hummingbird-size moss-covered baskets (opposite) are the perfect accents for your holiday centerpiece. Fill them with painted wooden eggs splashed with gold paint, or nestle a few chocolates in each basket.

Galax grows wild as a ground cover in Southern woodlands. You'll also find it at florists' shops, where the glossy green foliage is prized for flower arrangements. The netted veining and frilled edges of the leaves offer a distinctive texture that we've highlighted with gold and silver to create this gilded galax globe (right).

Gilded cornucopias (see next page), made from a cluster of magnolia leaves, were inspired by the candy-filled paper cones with which the Victorians decorated their trees. Stuff them with colorful tissue paper or dried flowers and hang them on your tree, or use them as party favors.

Finally, lunaria, or money plant, pods glued to an egg-shaped piece of craft foam give an elegant twist to a natural "pinecone" (see page 73).

MOSS-COVERED BASKETS

Materials (for 1 basket):
sheet moss
low-melt hot-glue gun and glue sticks
1 (1¼-ounce) paper nut cup (for small
    basket) or 1 (3¼-ounce) paper
    nut cup (for large basket)
1 or 2 (14") lengths of grapevine

Working on a flat surface and with moss right side down, form a 7" circle of moss by overlapping edges of small pieces. (**Note:** For large basket, you will need a 9" circle of moss.) Apply glue to outer bottom surface of nut cup. Center cup on moss circle and press firmly to secure.

To form handle, twist lengths of grapevine together and bend to form a U shape. Glue ends to outside of cup. Apply glue to top rim of cup. Fold moss up sides of cup, and then down over rim. Split moss as required to pass around handles.

Moisten hands and mold moss around cup to shape outside of basket. Let dry.

A GLOBE OF GALAX LEAVES

Materials:
2" length of 16-gauge wire
thick white glue
4"-diameter craft foam ball
1 dozen galax leaves
waxed paper
small brush
ColorWorks® brass enamel spray paint
silver Treasure Gold®
1 yard (⅝"-wide) red ribbon (optional)

To form hanger for ball, bend wire into a hook. Coat straight end of wire with glue and insert in craft foam ball.

Remove stems from galax leaves. To flatten leaves and make them more flexible, place between 2 sheets of waxed paper and press with a hot iron.

To apply leaves to ball, hold by hanger and brush a layer of glue onto ball. Press leaves onto ball, working from bottom to top and overlapping edges. Gently pleat edges of leaves where necessary to make them lie flat, and apply extra glue to undersides of leaves where needed. Let glue dry.

Spray ball with brass paint and let dry. Rub with silver Treasure Gold® to highlight veins and edges of leaves. If desired, tie ribbon into bow at hanger.

Place 1 magnolia leaf over cone so that bottom of leaf wraps around tip of cone. Glue right edge of leaf to cone, leaving left edge free. Place second magnolia leaf so that right edge slips under free left edge of first leaf.

Glue right edge of second leaf to cone and then glue overlapping edge of first leaf over second leaf. Repeat with third leaf, gluing left edge over right edge of first leaf.

Allow to dry for several days. After leaves are thoroughly dry, spray entire cone, inside and out, with brass paint and let dry. (If leaves are not completely dry before being painted, the paint will flake off.) Lightly rub silver Treasure Gold® over surface of leaves, outside and inside where leaves extend above cone.

To make hanger, glue ends of ribbon to inside of cardboard cone.

LUNARIA PINECONES

Materials (for 1 ornament):
2" length of 16-gauge wire
low-melt hot-glue gun and glue sticks
1 (3¼"-tall) craft foam egg
60 lunaria seed pods
5" (1/16"-wide) gold cord
7" (3/8"-wide) ivory or gold
ribbon (optional)

To form hanger base, bend wire into a U shape. Apply glue to ends and insert wire into center of wide end of foam egg, leaving ½" of wire U sticking out of foam.

Gently rub each lunaria seed pod between fingertips to remove the 2 outer husks and seeds.

Apply a small amount of glue to upper edges of 5 pods. Holding foam egg by hanger base and beginning at smaller end of egg, cover bottom of egg with pods, overlapping edges as you work.

Apply a second round of overlapping pods just above the first row, making sure bottom ends of new pods cover tops of previous round. Repeat until egg is completely covered.

To form the hanger, thread gold cord through wire and knot ends. If desired, thread ivory or gold ribbon through wire and tie in a bow. ❧

MAGNOLIA-LEAF CORNUCOPIA

Materials:
manila folder or similar weight card stock
low-melt hot-glue gun and glue sticks
3 fresh magnolia leaves
ColorWorks® brass enamel spray paint
silver Treasure Gold®
⅓ yard (3/8"-wide) gold ribbon

Cut a 10"-diameter circle from manila folder. Cut circle in half. Roll half-circle to form a cone with a top diameter of about 2". Glue to secure.

Heirlooms for the Tree

You can create a charming turn-of-the-century family Christmas tree by embellishing it with lace-framed color copies of treasured photographs. Make these ornaments in multiples and give them to each member of the family to celebrate your heritage.

Materials (for 3 frames):
graph paper
scraps of mat board
craft knife
½-yard lengths of assorted heavy
    laces
craft glue
cotton twine
1 (8-ounce) jar of ivory lace Blooming
    Visions liquid bisque
small paintbrushes
3 large paper clips
wire cutters
antique white spray paint
Florentine gold Treasure Gold®
transparent tape
photocopies of photographs to fit
    2" x 3" opening
scraps of ¼"-wide ribbon (optional)

To create the frames shown here, draw 1 (3½" x 4½") rectangle and 2 (4" x 5") rectangles on graph paper. Draw a 2" x 3" rectangle in the center of each to serve as the opening for the photograph. Transfer patterns to wrong side of mat board and cut out using craft knife. For each mat, cut a matching backing piece from mat board. (If you prefer, have a frame shop cut the mats.)

To complete 1 frame, experiment to find the best arrangement of lace. Some frames may look better if the lace is cut in half lengthwise or into smaller pieces. Glue lace in place. If desired, glue twine around outer edges of front. Let dry.

Coat front and edges of frame with liquid bisque. Be careful not to fill the openings in the lace with bisque. Remove excess bisque by dabbing with a dry paintbrush. Let dry.

To make hanger, cut a 2" U shape from 1 end of paper clip. Glue to wrong side of frame at center top.

Spray frame and backing with antique white paint. Let dry. Rub Treasure Gold® on frame to highlight as desired. Tape photocopy to wrong side of frame; glue backing in place. Repeat to complete remaining frames. If desired, tie ¼"-wide ribbon in bow at base of each hanger.

Note: To obtain the antique look of a sepia-toned print, have your local copy shop color-copy your photograph in brown. 🍎

Season's Greetings in a Folded Puzzle Purse

This Christmas, delight your friends with a modern adaptation of a historic greeting card. The puzzle purse, or rebus card, was a popular 18th-century valentine: a single sheet of paper made both the card and the envelope. Opened, our yuletide rebus has the effect of a paper kaleidoscope embellished with colorful images and cheerful verses.

To form the basic card, begin with a 12-inch square of 65-pound artist's paper. Using a pencil, lightly mark the center of the square. Fold all four corners to meet in the center; crease. Fold the resulting flapped corners to meet in the center again; crease (see diagram).

Open the second set of folds. Using rubber stamps with embossing ink and powder, follow manufacturer's instructions to decorate this area. Use colored pencils to fill in parts of the stamped and embossed image.

Open a small window in the center of the card by folding back the original corners. Stamp another design or write your personal greeting here. You might want to use a special embossing pen or a glue pen to emboss your handwritten verse. When finished, close the window and the second set of folds. The written greeting and stamped images are now enclosed in their own "envelope."

Address the envelope on the flat front side. If desired, emboss an image on the front as well to give your friends a hint of the good tidings inside. Seal the center back flaps with a purchased self-adhesive sticker. ❦

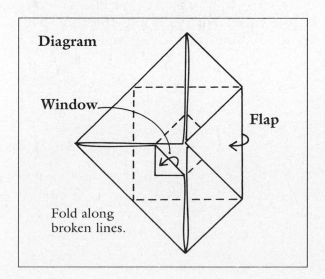

Diagram

Window

Flap

Fold along broken lines.

Jolly Elves Ring This Wreath

Able to spare but a few minutes away from the toy shop, Santa's elves posed for this happy wreath. Displayed here over a fresh evergreen wreath, our toy-making bunch carries a merry assortment of dollhouse-size gifts. To make the wreath, glue this clothespin crew to a metal ring, which you can find at a craft store among the macramé supplies.

Materials:
31 round clothespins
acrylic paints: black, white, red, and colors to coordinate with ribbons
16 (12"-long) 6-mm tan chenille wires
hot-glue gun and glue sticks
4 (1-yard) lengths of 1½"-wide ribbon in assorted plaids
5½ yards (¼"-wide) red satin ribbon
scrap of green felt
31 (5-mm) red pom-poms
12" metal ring
miniature toys

On round clothespins, paint elf faces. Using colors to coordinate with ribbons, paint striped leggings on each elf.

Cut chenille wires in half. Wrap 1 piece around each clothespin to form elf arms. Secure wire at back with a small drop of glue.

Cut plaid ribbons into 31 (4") pieces to make elf aprons. Fold ribbon pieces in half, matching cut edges. Cut a ½"-long rounded slit out of each fold. Fit 1 apron over each elf's head through cut. Tie red ribbon over apron to make belt. Trim ends of red ribbon at an angle.

From felt, cut 16 (1½") squares. Cut each square in half on the diagonal. To make hats, fold each triangle in half so that the long side meets itself. Put a spot of glue on an elf's head and set hat in place, positioning seam at back. Glue a pom-pom to pointed tip of hat. Arrange and glue elves shoulder to shoulder in a circle on top of metal ring.

Arrange miniature toys in the arms of some elves. When satisfied with the arrangement, glue toys in place. 🍎

Festive Fashion Accents to Snip and Glue

Change a simple outfit into a merry Christmas fashion when you add these miniature collages to button covers and earrings. Scraps of construction paper, shiny sequins, metallic confetti, and bright beads make up the holiday designs.

Use toothpicks or tweezers to help position the pieces, gluing each in place with a small dot of Mod Podge®.

SEQUIN WREATHS

Materials (for 4 button covers and 1 pair of earrings):
patterns on page 153
scrap of white paper
scraps of construction paper:
  white, red
pinking shears
gloss Mod Podge®
toothpick
cuticle scissors
¾ yard of green sequin strand
72 red seed beads
small paintbrush
acrylic matte sealer
craft glue
4 (⅝") blank button covers
1 set of earring clips or posts
  and backs

Transfer patterns to white paper. Lay pattern sheet on top of construction paper and, treating both papers as 1, use appropriate scissors to cut through layers along lines.

From white, use pinking shears to cut 12 bases. Apply a small amount of Mod Podge® with toothpick to 6 pieces and glue a second piece on top of each. Do not align points.

From red, use cuticle scissors to cut 6 bows and 6 knots.

Around outer edge of each base, glue sequins to form wreath. Glue 1 bow to top of each wreath. Glue 1 knot to center of each bow. Referring to photograph for placement, glue seed beads in sets of 3 around wreath.

Use paintbrush to apply several coats of Mod Podge® to completed collages and to backs of bases. Let dry between coats. Finish with 1 coat of sealer. Using craft glue, attach 1 wreath to each button cover and earring.

Above: Gift cards make a stylish presentation for a set of collage button covers or earrings. Following manufacturer's instructions, use fusible web to bond a fabric scrap to a 3- x 7½-inch piece of lightweight cardboard for the button covers or to a 3- x 4-inch piece for the earrings. Trim edges with pinking shears. Use a hole punch to start slits into which the button cover clasps and earring backs fit.

PAPER COLLAGE NATIVITY AND ANGELS

Materials (for 4 button covers and 1 pair of earrings):
patterns on page 153
scrap of white paper
scraps of construction paper: black, navy, yellow, white, blue, flesh, brown
pinking shears
gloss Mod Podge®
toothpick
cuticle scissors
hole punch
ballpoint pens: black, red
5-mm silver star sequins
½" metallic star confetti
⅝" silver and gold leaf sequins
seed beads in assorted colors
small paintbrush
acrylic matte sealer
craft glue
4 (⅝") blank button covers
1 set of earring clips or posts and backs

Transfer all patterns to white paper. Lay pattern sheet on top of construction paper and, treating both papers as 1, use appropriate scissors to cut through layers along lines.

From black and navy paper, use pinking shears to cut 6 bases each. Apply a small amount of Mod Podge® with toothpick to black pieces and glue 1 navy piece on top of each. Do not align points.

Referring to patterns for colors, use cuticle scissors to cut Nativity pieces.

From flesh-colored paper, use a hole punch to make 5 circles for faces. Using cuticle scissors, trim 1 circle to proper scale for baby's face. Using ball point pens, add details to each face.

From brown paper, use pinking shears to cut a narrow serrated strip for stable roof on Mary-and-baby button cover. Cut tiny scraps of yellow and brown paper for hay. For crown button cover, stack 1 crown on top of the other. Do not align points.

Referring to photograph, assemble collages on navy sides of bases. Apply small amount of Mod Podge® with toothpick to glue sequins, confetti, and beads onto collage. Use paintbrush to apply several coats of Mod Podge® to completed collages and to backs of bases. Let dry between coats. Finish with 1 coat of sealer. Using craft glue, attach 1 Nativity collage to each button cover and 1 angel to each earring. ❧

Quilted Santas Skirt the Tree

With button eyes, pom-pom noses, and snowy beards of quilted curls, six simple Santa faces add up to one tree skirt with lots of charm. Each Santa panel consists of eight right triangles stitched together to form one large triangle. The faces are painted, so there's no time-consuming appliqué or tricky piecing required.

Materials:
pattern and diagram on page 152
1/3 yard (45"-wide) red pindot
1/3 yard (45"-wide) green
  pindot
2 yards (45"-wide) muslin
threads to match
water-soluble fabric marker
light flesh fabric paint
12 (5/8") black buttons
1 1/3 yards of polyester batting
white quilting thread
1 1/2 yards (1/2"-wide) double-fold bias
  tape to match muslin
6 small red pom-poms
hot-glue gun and glue sticks
2/3 yard (1/4"-wide) cream satin
  ribbon

Note: Add 1/4" seam allowance to pattern.

Transfer pattern to fabrics and cut the following: From red pindot, cut 6 triangles; reverse pattern and cut 6. From green pindot, cut 6 triangles; reverse pattern and cut 6. From muslin, cut 12 triangles; reverse pattern and cut 12.

Referring to diagram, stitch 8 triangles together to make 1 Santa. Repeat to make 5 more. Referring to photograph, stitch Santas together to make skirt. (Do not join last Santa to first. This will be skirt opening.) Trim seams to 1/8" and press toward darker fabric. Trim points of hats to make opening for tree trunk.

On each muslin section of skirt: Referring to photograph, draw face, mustache, and beard curls, using water-soluble fabric marker. Paint face with fabric paint. Sew on button eyes.

Using pieced top as pattern, cut backing from muslin, adding 1" all around outside edge. Stack backing (right side down), batting, and pieced top (right side up). Baste through all layers. Using

white quilting thread, quilt around face and along lines for mustache and beard curls; stitch in-the-ditch between each Santa and where muslin joins pindot sections.

Trim batting (but not backing) to edges of pieced top. To bind lower edge of tree skirt, fold excess backing to right side of top, tuck under raw edge of muslin, and whipstitch. Bind trunk opening and opening edges with bias tape.

To finish, hot-glue 1 pom-pom in center of each mustache. To make ties, cut ribbon in half and stitch 1 piece to each side of top back. ❧

Cross-Stitch a Candy Calendar

Most children are restless with anticipation around the Christmas holiday. This Candy Countdown Calendar will help them count the days until St. Nick finally arrives. A sweet treat each day will make the long wait easier to swallow.

Materials:
chart and color key on page 154
1 (7" x 46") piece of 14-count white Aida cloth
2 skeins DMC floss #699
5⅓ yards (⅛"-wide) green satin ribbon
large-eyed needle
3⅓ yards (⅞"-wide) plaid ribbon
1 (7" x 46") piece of lightweight fusible interfacing
1 (8" x 47") piece of green fabric
threads to match ribbon and fabric
9" bellpull hanger rod
24 pieces of peppermint candy

To prepare Aida cloth, baste straight across material 7" from 1 short end. Beginning at basting thread and running length of fabric, baste 2½" in from each side (you will use these lines for centering the numbers).

Using 3 strands of floss, center and stitch verse inside 7" square at top of Aida cloth. Using 2 strands of floss, stitch the number "1" 2 threads down from the horizontal basting thread, centering on left vertical basting thread. Stitch the number "2" 2 threads below the number "1," centering on right vertical basting line. Stitch the number "3" 31 threads below the number "1," centering on left basting line. Continue stitching remaining numbers in same manner.

Cut ⅛"-wide satin ribbon into 24 (8") lengths. Using large-eyed needle, thread ribbon through Aida cloth, centering ribbon 2 threads down from each number. To finish front of calendar, measure length of ribbon needed for 1 vertical edge; cut

2. Place 1 length of plaid ribbon along each side, aligning outside edges. Stitch along inside edges. Measure length of ribbon needed for 1 horizontal edge; cut 3. Place length of plaid ribbon along top and bottom of Aida cloth, aligning outside edges. Stitch along inside edges. Align lower edge of remaining length of plaid ribbon along horizontal basting thread. Stitch along both long edges.

For backing, follow manufacturer's directions to center and fuse interfacing to wrong side of green fabric. Turn all edges of fabric under ½" toward interfacing and press. With wrong sides facing, stitch calendar front to back along outside edges, leaving open at sides of top plaid ribbon piece for bellpull rod. Insert rod through casing and tie remaining length of green satin ribbon to either side for hanger. Attach 1 piece of peppermint candy below each number by tying ribbon in a bow around 1 end of candy wrapper at twist. ❧

A Tisket, a Tasket,
Some Little Christmas Baskets

These little baskets are so easy and inexpensive to make, you'll want to craft lots of them to fill with candy or other treats. Give them to neighbors, friends at the office, or your children's teachers. Or use them as party favors and send each guest home with something sweet. The baskets will also look festive hanging on the branches of your Christmas tree.

Materials (for 1 basket):
1 disposable plastic bathroom cup
narrow-necked bottle
craft glue
paintbrush
2 coffee filters
rubber band
9" length of heavy florist's wire
needle-nose pliers
ice pick
red spray paint
⅔ yards (⅜"-wide) white opalescent
   ribbon

Invert cup over neck of bottle to support cup as you work. Brush glue on bottom of cup. Handling 2 coffee filters as 1, center filters over bottom of cup and press firmly.

Brush sides of filters with glue, soaking them thoroughly; press firmly with brush to make filters adhere to sides of cup. Gather glue-soaked filters around rim of cup and hold in place with rubber band, just below rim of cup. Redistribute fullness of filters as necessary to obtain even gathers. Shape edge of coffee filters to make ruffle. Let basket dry thoroughly.

To form handle, bend wire into a U shape. Using needle-nose pliers, form a hook at each end. With an ice pick, carefully punch 1 hole on each side of cup rim, making sure hole is large enough to receive wire. (Plastic is brittle and may split if you try to force the wire through.) Carefully insert hooked ends of wire through holes and crimp hooks closed.

Remove rubber band below ruffle. Spray entire basket, inside and out, with red paint. Let dry. To finish, tie ribbon in a bow just below ruffle. ❧

83

Knit Some Merry Mittens
For St. Nick to Fill

These whimsical stockings will hold more than a handful of goodies. They're easy to knit and fun to fill—save something special for the thumb.

Materials (for 2 stockings):
worsted-weight acrylic (247-yd. skein):
   1 skein each yellow, blue, red (for blue mitten); 1 skein each yellow, red, green (for red mitten)
size 8 knitting needles (or size to obtain gauge)
stitch markers
2 stitch holders
tapestry needle

Finished Size: Approximately 12" long.
   Gauge: 9 sts and 12 rows = 2" in St st.
   Blue mitten: Cuff: With yellow, cast on 80 sts. Work in k 2, p 2 ribbing for 12 rows. *Row 13:* P across. *Row 14:* * K 8, inc 1 st in next st, rep from * across, ending with k 8 = 88 sts. Cut yarn. *Row 15:* Join blue, k 42, sl marker on needle, inc 1 st in each of next 5 sts, sl marker on needle = 10 sts between markers for thumb, k to end of row.
   Thumb: Odd-numbered rows 1-19: P across. *Even-numbered rows 2-20:* K across to first marker, sl marker, k 1, inc 1 in next st, k across to 2 sts before next marker, inc 1 in next st, k 1, sl marker, k across to end of row. *Row 21:* P 42, sl these 42 sts onto first holder, p 28 thumb sts, sl next 43 sts onto 2nd holder. Work back and forth in St st on 28 thumb sts for 12 rows. Cut yarn. *Row 34:* Join red, k 2 tog, k across to last 2 sts, k 2 tog. *Row 35:* P across. *Row 36:* K across, dec 1 st at beginning, middle, and end of row. *Rows 37-42:* Rep rows 35 and 36. Cut yarn, leaving a tail. Using tapestry needle, thread yarn tail through remaining sts, pull up tightly, and secure. Sew thumb seam.
   Hand: Row 1: Put sts from 2nd holder back on needle. Join blue, p across. *Row 2:* K 43, put sts from first holder back on needle (joining the 2 halves flush), k 42. Work even in St st for 17 rows.

Shape hand: Row 1: K 2 tog, k 40, sl 2nd st on left needle over first st and off needle to dec, k 40, k 2 tog. *Even-numbered rows 2-20:* P across. *Row 3:* K 2 tog, k 39, sl 2nd st off left needle, k 38, k 2 tog. *Row 5:* K 2 tog, k 37, sl 2nd st off left needle, k 37, k 2 tog. *Row 7:* K 2 tog, k 36, sl 2nd st off left needle, k 35, k 2 tog. Cut yarn. *Row 9:* Join red, k 2 tog, k 34, sl 2nd st off left needle, k 34, k 2 tog. *Row 11:* K 2 tog, k 33, sl 2nd st off left needle, k 32, k 2 tog. *Row 13:* K 2 tog, k 31, sl 2nd st off left needle, k 31, k 2 tog. *Row 15:* K 2 tog, k 30, sl 2nd st off left needle, k 29, k 2 tog. *Row 17:* K 2 tog, k 28, sl 2nd st off left needle, k 28, k 2 tog. *Row 19:* K 2 tog twice, k 24, sl 2nd st off left needle, k 1, sl 2nd st off left needle, k 23, k 2 tog twice. *Row 21:* K 2 tog twice, k 20, sl 2nd st off left needle, k 1, sl 2nd st off left needle, k 21, k 2 tog twice. *Row 22:* P across. Cut yarn, leaving a tail. With tapestry needle, thread yarn tail through remaining sts, pull up tightly, and secure. Sew mitten seam.
   Hanger: With yellow, cast on 5 sts. *Row 1:* (K 1, p 1) around. *Row 2:* (P 1, k 1) around. Rep rows 1 and 2 until piece measures 4". Bind off in pattern. Fold hanger in half and stitch ends inside stocking cuff above thumb.
   Red mitten: Work as for blue mitten, using yellow for cuff and hanger, red for hand and thumb, and green for tips of thumb and hand.

Knitting Abbreviations
dec—decrease(ing)
inc—increase (k in front and back of next st)
k—knit
p—purl
rep—repeat
sl—slip
st(s)—stitch(es)
St st—stockinette stitch (k 1 row, p 1 row)
tog—together

Celestial Ornaments

our gifts will sparkle like the heavens when adorned with these lamé ornaments. They're made using a simplified version of a Japanese art form in which a picture is created in relief with cardboard and padded fabric.

Materials:
patterns on page 150-51
lightweight cardboard (cardboard used in packaging shirts is good)
lightweight batting
craft glue
scraps of lamé fabric: gold, silver, purple
scrap of white fabric
permanent markers: black, green
gold thread
stiff silver string

Transfer patterns to cardboard and batting and cut out. Glue 1 piece of batting to each corresponding piece of cardboard. Referring to photograph, place shapes on scraps of lamé, batting side down, and cut out, adding ½" beyond edges of cardboard. Clip at corners and around curves. Fold fabric to backs of shapes and glue. Trim excess fabric.

Referring to photograph, for moon ornament, glue 1 cheek to each moon face; then glue 1 moon face to each moon backing. Cut out eyes from white fabric scrap. Add details with permanent markers. Glue 1 eye to each moon face. For hanger, fold 9" length of gold thread in half and glue ends to back of 1 side at top. Glue both sides together, aligning moon faces.

For sun ornament, glue 1 circle to each pointed backing. Glue 3 (1½") lengths of silver string between each point on back of 1 side. Glue hanger to back of 1 side. Align sides and glue together.

For star, glue 4 (3½"-4½") lengths of silver string to back of 1 side at bottom between points. Attach hanger as for moon. Align sides and glue together.

Note: Hold shapes together with clothespins as glue dries. Or, if you prefer, place shapes between books. ❧

86

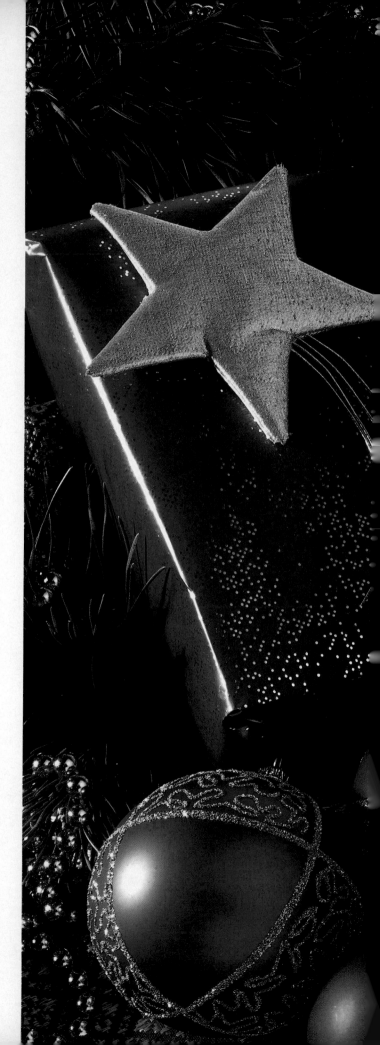

Stitch a Ribbon - Wreath Nightshirt

*F*or the night before Christmas and all through the month, bedtime can be fun time for your little one. Bright grosgrain ribbons and berry buttons make this a fast and simple project to sew for an early surprise. To make this a really comfortable gift, be sure to buy a roomy T-shirt that is a few sizes larger than the child would usually wear.

Materials:
2 yards (⅞"-wide) green grosgrain
  ribbon
liquid ravel preventer
T-shirt board or cardboard
white T-shirt
fabric glue
15 (⅜") red buttons
⅓ yard (⅝"-wide) red grosgrain
  ribbon
threads to match ribbons

From green ribbon, cut 12 (5½") pieces. Cut V-shaped notches at both ends of each piece. Apply liquid ravel preventer to cut ends. Fold each piece in half to form a V. Using green thread, edgestitch close to fold.

Place cardboard inside T-shirt to prevent glue from soaking through to back of shirt. On center front of T-shirt, arrange folded green ribbons in a circle to form a wreath. Place folds at center of wreath with tips just touching. Glue folded ends in place, leaving notched ends free. Referring to photograph for placement, position and glue buttons in groups of three around wreath. After glue has dried, remove cardboard.

Set sewing machine for a wide and tight zigzag. Using green thread, stitch around center of wreath over folded edges of green ribbon. Using red thread, handstitch buttons in place.

Make a bow from red ribbon. Trim ends at an angle and apply liquid ravel preventer. Referring to photograph and using red thread, handstitch bow to wreath. ❧

A Quick-and-Easy Stocking to Sew

Prequilted muslin embellished with trendy jumbo rickrack and bright buttons makes this playful stocking a simple-to-sew project. Tied to the footboard of a child's bed or hung on the mantel, it is sure to hold a merry surprise on that special morning.

Materials:
pattern on page 155
paper
pencil
ruler
½ yard (45"-wide) prequilted muslin
water-soluble fabric marker
23" green jumbo rickrack
26" red jumbo rickrack
threads to match fabric and rickracks
11 (½") yellow star buttons
6 (¾") red round buttons with 4 holes

Note: Add ¼" seam allowance to pattern.

Transfer stocking toe pattern and placement lines for rickrack and buttons to paper. Extend leg 11". Mark rickrack placement lines 2¾" apart on leg, beginning 2⅞" from red rickrack line on pattern. Mark button placements between rickrack placement lines. On paper, draw a 2½" x 7¾" rectangle for stocking facing pattern.

From fabric, using pattern as a guide, cut 1 stocking front. Reverse pattern and cut 1 stocking back. Cut 2 stocking facings. Using fabric marker, transfer rickrack and button placements to right side of stocking front. Zigzag raw edges of stocking front, back, and facings.

From green rickrack, cut 1 (8") piece and 2 (7½") pieces. From red rickrack, cut 1 (10½") piece and 2 (7½") pieces.

To make hanger, fold 8" piece of green rickrack in half to form a loop. Tack loop to right side of stocking front at upper left edge. With right sides facing and raw edges aligned, sew 1 facing to stocking front along upper edge, catching raw

edge of rickrack loop in seam. Sew other facing to stocking back in same way. Fold facings to wrong side and tack in place.

Using matching thread, stitch 10½" piece of red rickrack to stocking front at line across toe. Alternate red and green rickrack along remaining lines and stitch in place. Referring to photograph for placement, handstitch star buttons at marked points. Using green thread, handstitch red buttons at marked points, making a cross with the threads.

To assemble stocking, with right sides facing and raw edges aligned, sew stocking front to back, leaving top edge open and keeping hanger free. Turn to right side. ❧

Beribboned Balls

These elegant Victorian-style ornaments are simple to assemble: there's nothing more to making them than pinning ribbon and fabric to a craft foam ball. For a more elaborate effect, you could replace the corsage pins with acrylic jewels or beads secured with dressmaker's pins.

GREEN VELVETEEN BALL

Materials:
pattern on page 151
scraps of green velveteen
dressmaker's pins
1 (3"-diameter) craft foam ball
white glue (optional)
1¼ yards (⅞"-wide) white ribbon
    with gold edge
1¼ yards (⅜"-wide) white ribbon
    with gold edge
9 (4-mm) gold beads
3 pearl-tipped corsage pins
2" (⅛"-wide) gold ribbon

Transfer pattern A to fabric and cut 6. Using dressmaker's pins, pin each section to craft foam ball at top and bottom, overlapping edges to cover craft foam. Smooth fabric edges and secure with white glue, if desired.

Twist 1 end of ⅞"-wide ribbon and secure to top of ball with dressmaker's pin. Make sure that ribbon is centered over 1 seam. Twist ribbon at center of ball and again at bottom, securing each twist with a pin. Continue twisting and pinning ribbon in same manner to cover alternate seams, dividing ball into thirds. After final twist, cut off excess ribbon, tuck end under, and pin.

Repeat with ⅜"-wide ribbon to cover remaining seams, twisting ribbon 3 times as shown in photograph. Before securing each twist with pin, thread a gold bead onto pin.

From remaining ⅜"-wide ribbon, make 3 small bows. With corsage pin, secure 1 bow over the center twist of each wide ribbon strip. (It is not necessary to remove dressmaker's pins at center twists.)

To make tail, cut a 4" piece of ⅞"-wide ribbon. Cut a V in each end. Twist ribbon in the middle and secure to bottom of ball with pin.

To make hanger, pin ends of 2" length of ⅛"-wide ribbon to top of ball.

WHITE MOIRÉ BALL

Materials:
pattern on page 151
scraps of white moiré
dressmaker's pins
1 (3"-diameter) craft foam ball
white glue (optional)
1¼ yards (⅞"-wide) red picot-edged
    ribbon
1¼ yards (⅝"-wide) red picot-edged
    ribbon
12 pearl-tipped corsage pins
2" (⅛"-wide) red satin
    ribbon

Follow instructions for Green Velveteen Ball, omitting bows and using corsage pins to hold all ribbon twists.

RED SATIN BALL

Materials:
pattern on page 151
scraps of red satin
dressmaker's pins
1 (3"-diameter) craft foam ball
white glue (optional)
1¼ yards (1"-wide) gold picot-edged
    ribbon
5 pearl-tipped corsage pins
½ yard (⅛"-wide) red satin
    ribbon

Transfer pattern B to fabric and cut 8. Placing a dressmaker's pin at each corner, pin triangles to ball, smoothing fabric to conform to shape and overlapping edges slightly. If desired, secure edges with white glue.

To cover "equator" of ball, twist 1 end of gold ribbon and pin at 1 of the points where 4

triangles meet in middle of ball. Bring ribbon around ball over center seam, twisting and pinning ribbon at each point where 4 triangles meet. When you reach beginning, cut off excess ribbon, twist end, and secure with dressmaker's pin.

To cover vertical seams, position remaining gold ribbon over 1 seam, twist 1 end of ribbon, and pin to top of ball. Twist ribbon at center of ball (over twist of horizontal ribbon) and again at bottom, securing each twist with dressmaker's pin.

Bring ribbon up over seam on opposite side of ball, twisting and pinning at center and top. Repeat to cover remaining vertical seams. Cut off excess ribbon, tuck end under, and pin. Adjust twists as necessary to achieve symmetry. At equator and bottom of ball, replace dressmaker's pins with corsage pins.

To make hanger, cut 2" length from red ribbon and pin ends to top of ball. With remaining red ribbon, make bow and pin to bottom of loop. 🍎

Sculpt Your Own Tabletop Angel

You'll create an heirloom when you make this beautiful angel. We've dressed her in colors inspired by 14th-century Italian frescoes, but you could use rich, jewel-toned satins if you prefer.

Materials:
patterns on page 153
2 (2-ounce) packages of translucent
   Sculpey III modeling compound
toothpicks
emery board or sandpaper
acrylic paints: light ivory, rose, light blue,
   black
paintbrushes: medium, fine
tracing paper
dressmaker's pins
pencil
1 (12"-tall) craft foam cone
22" length of 16-gauge wire
low-melt hot-glue gun and glue sticks
½ yard (45"-wide) pale green satin
1 yard (⅝"-wide) rose satin ribbon
threads to match fabric and ribbon
1 yard (⅜"-diameter) gold cord
18" (⅜"-wide) beige rayon
   cording
white glue
6" piece of gold gimp
12" piece of gold embroidery thread
3 (8½" x 11") sheets of heavy white
   paper
piece of heavy cardboard
awl or ice pick

Note: All seam allowances are ¼".

To make head and shoulders: From Sculpey, roll a 1⅛"-diameter ball for head; a cylinder ½" long and ⅝" in diameter for neck; and a cylinder 2½" long and ⅞" in diameter for shoulders.

Flatten 1 side of 2½"-long cylinder to form base of shoulders. Stack head, neck, and shoulders (see Diagram 1, page 94). With fingers or toothpick, smooth shapes together, rounding shoulders slightly (see Diagram 2).

To make face: Referring to Diagram 2, make balls for chin and cheeks and wedge for nose from Sculpey. Place features on face, flattening and smoothing to shape. Make hole for toothpick from bottom of shoulders into neck.

To make arms: From Sculpey, form a cylinder 2½" long and tapering from ½" in diameter at 1 end (elbow) to ⁵⁄₁₆" at other (fingertips). Flatten lower ½" to shape hand. To make thumb, roll a small amount of Sculpey into a small cylinder, flatten at 1 end, and attach to hand (see Diagram 3). Repeat to make other arm, reversing position of thumb. With toothpick, make a hole ½" deep at elbow end of each arm to receive wire.

Following manufacturer's instructions, bake head unit and arms. Let cool. Smooth pieces with emery board or sandpaper.

Paint arms, head, neck, and shoulders, using a mixture of 3 parts light ivory to 1 part rose. Let dry. Trace face pattern (Diagram 4) onto tracing paper. Make pin holes in pattern along lines of eyes, eyebrows, and mouth. Transfer to sculpted face by inserting point of pencil in each pin hole. Using fine paintbrush and referring to photograph, paint features. (You may want to practice painting features on paper first.)

To assemble angel: For body, cut 2½" from top of cone and discard. To attach arms, cut a 7" piece of wire and insert 1 end in 1 arm hole, securing with hot glue. Cut and bend 2 (2") pieces of wire into U shape and use as staples to secure remaining end of wire to top of cone. Repeat with remaining arm. To attach head unit, coat toothpick with hot glue and insert 1 end into hole in shoulders. Insert opposite end in top of cone.

To make dress: From green satin, cut 2 bodice pieces (bodice and lining), 1 (16½" x 10") rectangle (skirt), and 2 sleeves. Cut bodice and lining along center back fold. With right sides facing and raw edges aligned, stitch bodice and lining together along back opening and neckline. Turn and press. Fold bodice at shoulders and, with right sides facing and raw edges aligned, stitch each side seam through all 4 layers. Turn.

To make skirt, fold (16½" x 10") rectangle in half, with right sides facing and raw edges aligned, and stitch 10" edge. Turn. Gather 1 end. Pull skirt up over cone, adjust gathers to fit tightly around top of cone, and fasten off. Pin gathered edge of fabric to top edge of cone. Pull bodice on over arms and head. Secure with pins, covering gathers. To make sash, cut 1 (6½") piece from ribbon. Wrap around body, covering raw edge of bodice. Secure with pin at back. From gold cord, cut 1 (6½") piece. Place cord over ribbon and secure with pin at back. Turn under ¼" hem on skirt and, using hot-glue gun, glue to bottom edge of cone.

To make sleeves, turn under ¼" hem on bottom edge of 1 sleeve piece and baste. With right sides facing and raw edges aligned, stitch underarm seam. Turn. Loosely gather armhole of sleeve. Fold gathers under and secure to armhole of bodice, using hot glue. To make sleeve extensions, cut 2 (13") pieces each from ribbon and gold cord. Whipstitch 1 piece of cord to 1 edge of 1 ribbon strip. (This is front edge.) With right sides together, stitch raw edges of cord/ribbon unit together. Turn. Topstitch to enclose seam. Slipstitch back ribbon edges together to within 1½" of fold. Slip over 1 arm through opening, tuck ribbon under sleeve along front, and, using hot glue, secure extension to bottom edge of sleeve. Repeat for remaining sleeve extension.

To make hair, cut rayon cording into 3 (6") pieces and unravel. Apply white glue to top and back of head. Working from front to back, arrange sections across top of head and press into place. On back of head, angle sections toward crown for a natural effect.

To make halo, form gimp into circle, overlap ends, and glue to back of head. Tie gold embroidery thread around forehead.

To make wings: Fold sheets of paper in half widthwise. Transfer patterns to paper and cut out. On 1 half of each wing section, lightly trace solid lines on right side of paper and broken lines on wrong side. Reverse pattern to trace lines on other half of each wing section. Working on heavy cardboard, trace each solid line with awl or ice pick to score paper. Turn paper over and score broken lines. Stack wing sections and glue along top edges. Leave feather ends free to give a dimensional effect. With dressmaker's pin, secure to back of angel at waistband. 🍃

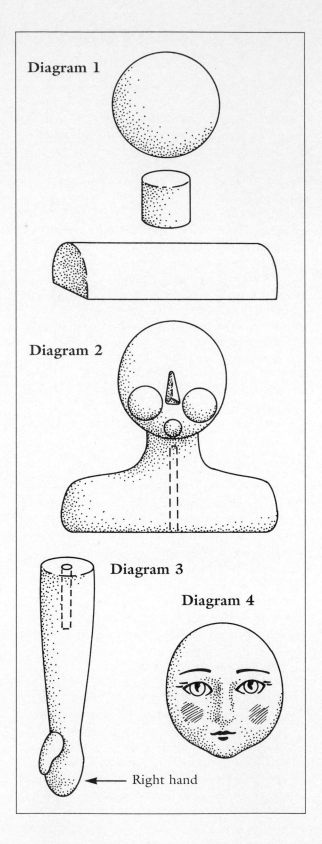

Diagram 1

Diagram 2

Diagram 3

Diagram 4

← Right hand

String a Garland Of Orange Swirls

Citrus and cinnamon are natural partners for a Christmas garland. Two oranges yield enough dried slices to make about two yards of garland. For home-drying instructions, see our recipe for Spice Mix on page 116. Waxing the dried orange slices preserves their warm amber color. During this process, the dried slices become pliable enough to twist into graceful spirals. The wax, when hardened, holds the shape and gives the twists a soft sheen.

Materials (for 2 yards of garland):
craft knife
14 dried orange slices
½ pound of paraffin blocks
75 (1½") cinnamon sticks
drill and ¹⁄₁₆" drill bit
large-eyed needle
2½ yards (10-pound)
  monofilament
90 (6-mm) gold sand beads

Using craft knife, cut from center of each slice to outer edge through rind. Follow manufacturer's instructions to melt paraffin. Holding 1 slice at cut edge, dip slice into paraffin. While wax is still soft, gently twist slice by pulling cut edges in opposite directions to form spiral. Carefully holding slice at waxed edge, dip orange twist into paraffin again. Set spiral-shaped slice aside; let wax harden. Repeat to wax and shape remaining slices.

Referring to photograph and using drill with ¹⁄₁₆" drill bit, make a hole for stringing through center of each cinnamon stick.

Thread needle with monofilament. Thread loose end of monofilament through and around first bead; knot to secure. Alternating beads and cinnamon sticks, string 6 beads and 5 sticks on monofilament, beginning and ending with a bead. Then string 1 orange swirl on monofilament. To secure swirl, pull needle through rind about ½" from cut. Loop monofilament around outside edge of rind and bring needle through same hole

Above: Orange-and-cinnamon garland wraps a simple topiary. This tabletop tree is a craft foam cone covered with green sheet moss. To make dried moss more manageable, enclose it in a large plastic bag with a couple of teaspoons of water and shake vigorously.

again; pull tight. Take monofilament across orange swirl. Pull needle through rind about ½" from cut on that side of swirl and loop around and through rind again. Continue to string beads, cinnamon sticks, and orange swirls until all are used. Knot end of monofilament around last bead to secure.

95

Celebrations
from
the Kitchen

A Splendid Setting For a Simple Meal

While it's the people who make the party, the setting and the menu go a long way toward creating the proper mood. The centerpiece shown here strikes a note of splendid elegance, and the meal is equally elegant—but simple. In fact, this menu proves that recipes need not be complicated nor dishes elaborately garnished in order to make a beautiful presentation. The colors of the foods themselves and their arrangement on the plate appeal artfully to the eye.

You can assemble the topiaries about a week ahead. Prepare the soup base, Roasted Garlic-Chive Butter, salad dressing, and dessert in the days leading up to the party. The rest of the meal can be ready in approximately an hour, leaving you free to relax and enjoy your guests.

MENU FOR SIX
Artichoke-Shrimp Bisque
Cracked Pepper Steak
with
Roasted Garlic-Chive Butter
Roasted Potato Medley
Walnut-Goat Cheese Salad
with
Orange Vinaigrette
Double-Chocolate Angel Food Torte

Left: Pomegranate-studded boxwood topiaries in brass urns create a spectacular setting for the meal. The tabletop trees are tall enough not to block your guests' views of each other. A length of silk that picks up the china pattern and a low bowl filled with pomegranates provide a visual link between the two trees.

99

ARTICHOKE-SHRIMP BISQUE

¼ cup butter or margarine
¼ cup all-purpose flour
3 cups chicken broth
1½ cups milk
⅛ teaspoon salt
¼ teaspoon white pepper
⅛ teaspoon ground nutmeg
⅛ teaspoon hot sauce
1½ cups half-and-half
1 (14-ounce) can artichoke hearts, drained and chopped
2 (7-ounce) cans tiny shrimp, drained

Melt butter in a heavy Dutch oven over low heat; add flour, stirring until smooth. Cook 1 minute, stirring constantly. Gradually add chicken broth and milk; cook over medium heat, stirring constantly, until mixture is thickened and bubbly. Stir in salt and next 3 ingredients; cover and chill 8 hours, if desired. Stir in half-and-half and remaining ingredients; cook over low heat until thoroughly heated. Yield: 8 cups.

CRACKED PEPPER STEAK WITH ROASTED GARLIC-CHIVE BUTTER

2 teaspoons cracked pepper
½ teaspoon garlic powder
½ teaspoon salt
1 (3-inch-thick) New York strip steak, trimmed (2½ pounds)
¼ cup butter or margarine, melted
Roasted Garlic-Chive Butter
Garnish: fresh chives

Combine first 3 ingredients; press evenly on steak. Cook steak in butter in a cast-iron skillet over medium heat 2 minutes on all sides. Bake at 450° for 25 to 27 minutes or until desired degree of doneness. Remove from oven; let stand 10 minutes. Slice and serve with Roasted Garlic-Chive Butter. Garnish, if desired. Yield: 6 servings.

Roasted Garlic-Chive Butter:

2 heads garlic
1½ tablespoons olive oil
¼ cup water
¾ cup butter or margarine, softened
1 tablespoon chopped fresh or frozen chives

Cut garlic heads in half crosswise, and place in a shallow pan. Drizzle with olive oil. Add water to pan; cover and bake at 450° for 20 minutes. Uncover and bake an additional 10 minutes. Let cool. Remove skins, and finely chop garlic. Combine garlic, butter, and chives; cover and chill. Yield: ¾ cup.

Above: Ingredients favored by creative chefs, such as roasted garlic and goat cheese, bring the latest culinary trends into your kitchen with Cracked Pepper Steak with Roasted Garlic-Chive Butter, Roasted Potato Medley, and Walnut-Goat Cheese Salad with Orange Vinaigrette.

Above: Instead of serving plates from the kitchen, arrange the dishes on a sideboard and let your guests serve themselves. This informal approach lets you join the party.

ROASTED POTATO MEDLEY

3 sweet potatoes, peeled and
  cut into ½-inch slices (about ½
  pound)
5 Irish potatoes, peeled and cut into
  ½-inch slices (about 1½ pounds)
3 tablespoons olive oil
1 tablespoon chopped fresh thyme or
  1 teaspoon dried thyme
½ teaspoon salt
½ teaspoon cracked pepper

Place potatoes in a single layer in a lightly greased 15- x 10- x 1-inch jellyroll pan; brush both sides with olive oil. Bake at 500° on bottom oven rack for 8 to 10 minutes on each side or until tender. Sprinkle with thyme, salt, and pepper. Serve immediately. Yield: 6 servings.

WALNUT-GOAT CHEESE SALAD WITH ORANGE VINAIGRETTE

6 cups mixed baby lettuce or mixed
  salad greens
½ cup chopped walnuts, toasted
1 (6-ounce) package goat cheese,
  thinly sliced
  Orange Vinaigrette

Arrange lettuce, walnuts, and goat cheese on a serving plate; serve with Orange Vinaigrette. Yield: 6 servings.

Orange Vinaigrette:

¼ cup orange juice
3 tablespoons white wine vinegar
⅛ teaspoon salt
⅛ teaspoon ground white pepper
½ cup vegetable oil
¼ cup olive oil

Combine orange juice and next 3 ingredients in container of an electric blender. With motor running, gradually add oils in a slow steady stream, processing until blended. Yield: 1 cup.

Above: Create this culinary tour de force *with little more than a cake mix! Double-Chocolate Angel Food Torte starts with a packaged cake mix; layers of fluffy cream filling repeat the baked-in stripes of chocolate and vanilla.*

DOUBLE-CHOCOLATE ANGEL FOOD TORTE

1 (14.5-ounce) package angel food cake mix
2 tablespoons cocoa, sifted
¼ teaspoon chocolate flavoring
Chocolate Cream
Amaretto Cream

Prepare cake mix according to package directions; divide batter in half. Fold cocoa and chocolate flavoring into 1 portion. Spoon portions into separate zip-top plastic bags; snip ½ inch off corner of each bag. Pipe batter in lengthwise strips into an ungreased 15- x 10- x 1-inch jellyroll pan, alternating vanilla and chocolate batters. Bake at 375° for 10 minutes. Invert cake onto a wire rack; let cool in pan, upside down, 30 minutes.

Remove cake from pan; cut 2 (7-inch) circles from one side of cake, leaving a 15- x 2-inch strip. Place 1 circle in bottom of an 8-inch springform pan; set aside remaining circle. Carefully slice remaining cake strip lengthwise in half, and arrange around sides of pan. Spread half of Chocolate Cream onto cake in prepared pan. Top with half of Amaretto Cream; cover and chill remaining Amaretto Cream. Add remaining Chocolate Cream, carefully spreading to sides of pan; top with remaining cake circle. Cover and chill at least 8 hours. Remove rim of pan, and spread reserved Amaretto Cream around sides of torte. Yield: 1 (8-inch) torte.

Chocolate Cream:

  2 **cups whipping cream, divided**
  1 **cup semisweet chocolate morsels**
  1 **teaspoon vanilla extract**

Combine 1 cup whipping cream, chocolate morsels, and vanilla in a heavy saucepan; cook over low heat until chocolate melts. Let cool. Cover and chill 8 hours.

Combine chocolate mixture and remaining whipping cream in a large bowl; beat at high speed with an electric mixer until soft peaks form. Yield: 2⅔ cups.

Amaretto Cream:

1½ **cups whipping cream**
  1 **cup vanilla-flavored morsels**
  ¼ **cup amaretto**

Combine whipping cream and morsels in a heavy saucepan; cook over low heat until morsels melt. Stir in amaretto; let cool. Cover and chill 8 hours. Beat at high speed with an electric mixer until soft peaks form. Yield: 2⅔ cups.

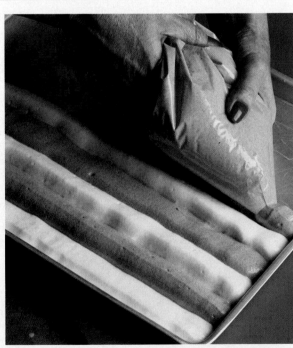

Above: Fill separate zip-top bags with chocolate and vanilla cake batter, cut a hole in one corner of the bag, and pipe batter in alternating strips onto the jellyroll pan.

Above: Cut two 7-inch circles from the cake for the top and bottom layers; then slice the remaining strip in half lengthwise. Use these halves to line the sides of the pan.

Above: The container that holds the topiary will determine whether the effect is dressy or casual: A terra-cotta pot, a stoneware crock, or a wicker basket would set an informal tone, while a silver champagne bucket or a brass planter yields a formal look. Be sure to embellish the topiary with ribbons and fruit or ornaments to harmonize with the container.

TOPIARY CENTERPIECE

Materials (for 1 topiary):
1 (4-pound) container plaster of Paris
1 thumbtack or small nail
1 (28"-long) ⅝"-diameter wooden
   dowel
florist's tape
green spray paint
large bucket
paint paddle or wooden spoon
spray adhesive
sheet moss
2 dome-shaped florist's foam holders
florist's wire
boxwood, cut in 3" to 10" lengths and
   soaked in water
dried pomegranates
upholstery tacks, gold and brass
   wire (optional)
ice pick
6" wooden florist's picks
bow
drapery tassel

Empty plaster of Paris from container; set aside. Push a thumbtack through center of bottom of empty 4-pound container; position dowel over tack, pressing down. Attach strips of florist's tape to top of container on either side of dowel to hold dowel in upright position; spray dowel with green paint. Set aside.

Pour 4 cups of water into a large bucket; gradually sprinkle 8 cups reserved plaster of Paris, 1 cup at a time, over water, and stir with a paint paddle until blended.

Quickly pour mixture into container fitted with dowel; set aside for plaster to harden, keeping dowel upright.

Coat dowel with spray adhesive; let dry 2 minutes. Tear sheet moss into small pieces; press onto adhesive on dowel.

Wire florist's foam holders together with florist's wire; soak in water 10 minutes. Press 1 end of foam holder onto top of dowel. Arrange boxwood in foam, forming a large ball.

Decorate pomegranates with upholstery tacks and wrap with gold and brass wire, if desired (see "Christmas Workroom," beginning on page 140). Make a hole in each pomegranate with an ice pick and insert blunt end of florist's pick. Push pomegranates randomly into topiary.

Place topiary in decorative container. Wire bow and drapery tassel to florist's picks and insert where dowel joins foam holders; cover visible plaster with sheet moss.

Tips: When mixing plaster of Paris, always add dry powder to water. Work quickly when pouring mixture into container fitted with dowel, so plaster doesn't set in mixing bucket.

  * To make sure the dowel is straight, position plastic container on a countertop under an overhanging wall cabinet; tape dowel to wall cabinet at a 90° angle to countertop.

  * Cut dowel shorter if topiary is to be used on a mantel or small table.

  * Purchase florist's foam holders from florists. (After using several times, replace florist's foam.)

  * Boxwood can be inserted in foam holders up to 1 week before the party. Cut flowers, such as carnations, can be added 2 days in advance.

How to Make a Boxwood Topiary

1. Add 8 cups of plaster of Paris, 1 cup at a time, to 4 cups of water and stir until blended.
2. Quickly pour plaster into prepared container. Set aside to harden, making sure dowel stays upright.
3. Coat dowel with spray adhesive and press small pieces of sheet moss onto dowel to cover.
4. Wire together two dome-shaped florist's foam holders and place on top of dowel.
5. Insert boxwood cuttings, working all the way around to create a globe of greenery. Add pomegranates on florist's picks and finish with a bow and drapery tassel at base of greenery.

From the Dessert Carts
Of Four Famous Chefs

The Christmas holidays are a time when nothing but the best will do. And this year, the rich, sweet aromas drifting from your kitchen can be the very best of the best. Below, four famous chefs from around the South have agreed to share favorite dessert recipes so that you can sample some of the delicacies for which they have become so well-known.

Chef Johnny Earles— *Criolla's, Grayton Beach*

Chef Johnny Earles, owner of Criolla's in Grayton Beach, Florida, near Seaside, knows how to roll with the tides. "Florida is a fun place to have a restaurant because so much of the flavor of the restaurant is based on the seasonality of things," Johnny says. The menu at Criolla's can change from one day to the next depending on what fresh ingredients are available.

This attitude of "going with the flow" translates to the atmosphere of the entire restaurant. Even the Coffee Crème Caramel that follows, while a staple on the menu, will take on a new "flavor" from day to day, depending on how Johnny garnishes it. Some of his suggestions include sprinkling the dessert with cinnamon and sugar or topping it with designs shaped from the caramel itself.

Tip: A vanilla bean can be reused. Rinse and dry the pod, and store in an airtight container; or make vanilla sugar by placing the dried pod in a sealed jar of sugar.

COFFEE CRÈME CARAMEL

1½ cups whipping cream
½ cup plus 2 tablespoons half-and-half
½ cup whole dark roast coffee beans
2 tablespoons Kahlúa or other coffee-flavored liqueur
2 tablespoons Frangelico or other hazelnut-flavored liqueur
2 tablespoons Irish cream liqueur
½ vanilla bean, split
2 large eggs
3 egg yolks
¼ cup plus 2 tablespoons sugar
1 cup sugar
½ cup plus 2 tablespoons water
Pinch of cream of tartar

Combine first 7 ingredients in a large saucepan; bring to a boil. Remove from heat; cover and let stand 10 minutes. Pour mixture through a large wire-mesh strainer into a large bowl, discarding solids; set aside.

Beat eggs, egg yolks, and ¼ cup plus 2 tablespoons sugar with a wire whisk until frothy. Gradually stir about one-fourth of hot mixture into egg mixture; add to remaining hot mixture. Chill.

Combine 1 cup sugar and remaining ingredients in a heavy saucepan; bring to a boil. Reduce heat, and simmer until mixture turns a light golden brown (about 10 minutes). Pour syrup to a depth of about ¼ inch into each of 6 (6-ounce) custard cups. Pour remaining hot syrup into thin, free-form designs onto buttered wax paper; set aside to cool.

Pour custard mixture into cups; place cups in a 13- x 9- x 2-inch pan, and cover each cup with foil. Pour hot water to a depth of 1 inch into pan. Bake at 350° for 50 minutes. Uncover and cool on a wire rack 30 minutes. Chill at least 4 hours. To serve, loosen edges with a thin-blade knife, and invert onto individual serving plates; top with caramel designs. Yield: 6 servings.

Above: As you prepare Coffee Crème Caramel, part of the dessert itself becomes the garnish. Thin, free-form caramel designs, made by pouring hot syrup onto buttered wax paper, create a golden framework to top the dessert.

Chef Paul Albrecht— *Pano's and Paul's, Atlanta*

Chef Paul Albrecht, co-owner of Pano's and Paul's in Atlanta, Georgia, began developing his culinary skills at the age of 14 when he entered a three-year chef apprenticeship in Munich, Germany. He went on to study French cuisine and moved to Geneva, Switzerland, where he worked in some of the best hotels and restaurants. Twenty-five years ago, Paul came to the United States.

Paul selected the dessert below because the hazelnuts remind him of wintertime and the festive aroma of roasting nuts.

FROZEN HAZELNUT SOUFFLÉ

1¼ cups sugar
1 cup water
9 large egg yolks
1 cup blanched hazelnuts, chopped and toasted
2 tablespoons cognac
2 tablespoons Frangelico or other hazelnut-flavored liqueur
1 cup whipping cream
Garnish: whipped cream

Cutting across width of roll, cut 6 pieces of aluminum foil long enough to fit around ⅓-cup ramekins, allowing a 1-inch overlap. Cut each piece in half, and fold each half lengthwise into thirds; lightly grease foil. Wrap 1 piece around outside of each of 12 ramekins, allowing foil to extend 2 inches above rim to form a collar. Secure with freezer tape or string, and set aside.

Combine sugar and water in a saucepan; bring to a boil, stirring until sugar dissolves, and cook 5 minutes. Beat egg yolks with a wire whisk until thick and pale. Gradually stir about one-fourth of hot mixture into yolks; add to remaining hot mixture, stirring constantly. Cook over medium heat, stirring constantly, until thickened. Remove from heat; beat until cool. Stir in hazelnuts and liqueurs.

Beat 1 cup whipping cream at medium speed with an electric mixer until soft peaks form; fold into egg yolk mixture. Spoon mixture evenly into each of 12 ramekins; freeze 8 hours or until firm. Remove collars before serving; garnish, if desired. Yield: 12 servings.

Above: Frozen Hazelnut Soufflé creates the illusion of a perfectly risen baked soufflé. Because it's prepared in ramekins, you can easily add decorative touches to the individual containers.

**Pastry Chef
Kirk Parks—
*Baby Routh, Dallas***

Kirk Parks, pastry chef at Baby Routh in Dallas, Texas, knows what people look for in a dessert. "I prefer to prepare desserts that melt in your mouth," he says. Kirk feels that people are more comfortable with old-fashioned desserts that are familiar. So Kirk will take a basic recipe and then "upscale" it. Kirk's recipe is a variation of a Baby Routh customer favorite.

CRANBERRY-CINNAMON CHEESE TART

1½   cups all-purpose flour
1   tablespoon sugar
½   teaspoon salt
½   cup shortening
¼ to ⅓ cup ice water
1   (12-ounce) package fresh or frozen cranberries
¾   cup sugar
2   tablespoons water
2   tablespoons rum
12   ounces cream cheese, softened
¼   cup butter, softened
¾   cup sugar
½   teaspoon ground cinnamon
  Grand Marnier Cream

Combine first 3 ingredients; cut in shortening with pastry blender until mixture is crumbly. Sprinkle ice water, 1 tablespoon at a time, evenly over surface; stir with a fork until dry ingredients are moistened. Shape into a ball.

Roll pastry into a 10½-inch circle on a lightly floured surface; place in a 10-inch tart pan. Trim edges, and prick bottom. Freeze 10 minutes. Place aluminum foil over pastry; fill with dried beans or pie weights. Bake at 325° for 45 minutes. (Crust will be very pale.) Remove foil, and let cool on a wire rack.

Above: Prepare Cranberry-Cinnamon Cheese Tart with cranberries during the holiday season, then substitute raspberries during the summer months.

Combine cranberries and next 3 ingredients in a heavy saucepan. Bring to a boil; reduce heat, and simmer, stirring constantly, 5 minutes or until mixture is thickened. Cool.

Beat cream cheese and butter at medium speed with an electric mixer until creamy; gradually add ¾ cup sugar and cinnamon, beating well. Spread evenly into prepared tart shell. Top with cranberry mixture. Serve with Grand Marnier Cream. Yield: 1 (10-inch) tart.

Grand Marnier Cream:

1   cup whipping cream
2   tablespoons sifted powdered sugar
1   tablespoon Grand Marnier or other orange-flavored liqueur

Combine all ingredients in a large mixing bowl; beat at medium speed with an electric mixer until whipping cream thickens, but is not stiff. Yield: 2 cups.

Above: Indulge yourself with a flavorful dish of Apple-and-Calvados Crisp. Add a dollop of Maple-Walnut Ice Cream to crown this spirited dessert.

110

Chef Jamie Shannon— *Commander's Palace, New Orleans*

"Extravagant" would be a good word to describe the types of desserts Chef Jamie Shannon likes to prepare for visitors to Commander's Palace in New Orleans, Louisiana. Jamie serves individual desserts with huge portions, because, he says, while people cannot possibly finish them, neither can they possibly forget them.

As Christmas approaches and the days grow cooler, even in New Orleans, Jamie says that he enjoys preparing apple recipes—especially apple desserts. Jamie studied for 2½ years at the Culinary Institute of America in the Hudson Valley, where Hudson Valley apples are, naturally, very popular. Therefore, during this special time of year, he enjoys serving something for which he has a special fondness. The following recipe is for an apple dessert that Jamie prepares for Commander's Palace.

APPLE-AND-CALVADOS CRISP WITH MAPLE-WALNUT ICE CREAM

    7   cups Gala apple slices
    ½   cup Calvados or other apple-
          flavored brandy, divided
    ¾   cup sugar
2 to 3 teaspoons ground cinnamon
    1   tablespoon lemon juice
    ½   cup raisins
    1   cup all-purpose flour
    ½   cup firmly packed brown sugar
    ½   cup butter
    ¼   teaspoon salt
        Maple-Walnut Ice Cream

Combine apples, ¼ cup Calvados, and next 3 ingredients; set aside. Cook raisins in boiling water 2 minutes; drain. Combine raisins and remaining Calvados; let stand 20 minutes. Stir raisin mixture into apple mixture; spoon in a 13- x 9- x 2-inch baking dish.

Place knife blade in food processor bowl; add flour and next 3 ingredients. Pulse until mixture is crumbly; sprinkle over apple mixture. Bake at 350° for 30 to 35 minutes. Serve with Maple-Walnut Ice Cream. Yield: 12 servings.

Maple-Walnut Ice Cream:

    3½ cups whipping cream, divided
    1½ cups milk, divided
    6   egg yolks
    2   large eggs, lightly beaten
    1   cup plus 3 tablespoons sugar
    ⅛   teaspoon salt
    ¾   cup maple syrup
    4   vanilla beans*
    ½   teaspoon ground nutmeg
    1   cup chopped walnuts, toasted

Combine 2 cups whipping cream and 1 cup milk in saucepan. Cook until heated (do not boil). Combine egg yolks and next 3 ingredients in top of a double boiler; bring water to a boil. Reduce heat to low; stir in whipping cream mixture, and cook, stirring constantly, 20 minutes. Remove from heat, and stir in remaining whipping cream, remaining milk, maple syrup, vanilla beans, and nutmeg. Cover and chill 3 hours. Remove and discard vanilla beans; stir in walnuts. Pour into freezer container of a 4-quart hand-turned or electric freezer. Freeze according to manufacturer's instructions. Yield: 2 quarts.

*1 teaspoon vanilla extract may be substituted.

Tips: To make Milk Punch Ice Cream, substitute ¾ cup brandy for maple syrup and omit walnuts.

*Gala apples have a tart-sweet flavor; Golden Delicious may be substituted.

*Make scoops of ice cream and place on baking sheets; freeze until ready to serve.

111

Gift Ideas

SPICED TEA PUNCH MIX

1 (22-ounce) jar instant
  orange-flavored breakfast drink
¾ cup instant tea with lemon
1½ cups sugar
1½ teaspoons ground cloves
1½ teaspoons ground cinnamon

Combine all ingredients; store in an airtight container. Yield: 5 cups.

Directions for gift recipe card: Combine ¾ cup Spiced Tea Punch Mix, ½ gallon unsweetened pineapple juice, ½ gallon apple juice, and 4 cups water in a Dutch oven. Bring to a boil; reduce heat, and simmer 15 minutes, stirring occasionally. Serve hot. Yield: 1¼ gallons.

SOURDOUGH WHEAT BREAD STARTER

1 package dry yeast
½ cup warm water (105° to 115°)
1 cup all-purpose flour
1 cup whole-wheat flour
3 tablespoons sugar
1 teaspoon salt
2 cups warm water (105° to 115°)

Combine yeast and ½ cup warm water in a 1-cup glass measure; let stand 5 minutes. Combine flours, sugar, and salt in a large, nonmetal bowl; gradually stir in 2 cups warm water. Add yeast mixture. Cover loosely with plastic wrap; let stand in a warm place (85°) for 72 hours, stirring 2 or 3 times daily. Remove two 1-cup portions to give as gifts; store remainder in refrigerator, stirring once a day. Replenish or use within 11 days. Yield: 3 cups.

Note: To replenish starter after removing 2 cups for gift portions, stir in ½ cup sugar, ½ cup all-purpose flour, ½ cup whole-wheat flour, and 1 cup milk. Refrigerate, stirring daily for 2 days; use within 14 days. Yield: 3 cups.

Directions for gift recipe card: Combine 1 package dry yeast and ¾ cup warm water (105° to 115°) in a large bowl; stir in ½ cup sourdough starter (at room temperature), 2 tablespoons sugar, 2 tablespoons vegetable oil, 1 teaspoon salt, 1 large egg, 1½ cups all-purpose flour, and 1½ cups whole-wheat flour. Turn dough out onto a floured surface, and knead 5 minutes. Place in a well-greased bowl, turning to grease top. Cover and let rise in a warm place (85°), free from drafts, 1½ hours or until doubled in bulk. Punch dough down, and shape into a loaf; place in a greased 9- x 5- x 3-inch loafpan. Cover and let rise in a warm place, free from drafts, about 30 minutes or until doubled in bulk. Bake at 375° for 25 to 30 minutes or until loaf sounds hollow when lightly tapped. Brush with melted butter. Yield: 1 loaf.

Replenish remaining ½ cup starter or use within 11 days.

BRAZIL NUT SENSATION

¾ cup all-purpose flour
¾ cup sugar
½ teaspoon baking powder
¼ teaspoon salt
1 (10-ounce) package Brazil nuts,
  chopped
4 (8-ounce) packages pitted dates,
  chopped
1 (10-ounce) jar maraschino cherries,
  drained and chopped
3 large eggs, lightly beaten
1 teaspoon vanilla extract

Grease a 9- x 5- x 3-inch loafpan; line bottom with wax paper, and set aside.

Combine first 4 ingredients; stir in nuts, dates, and cherries. Stir in eggs and vanilla. Spoon into prepared pan; bake at 300° for 1 hour and 45 minutes. Cool in pan on a wire rack 15 minutes; remove from pan. Peel off wax paper, and let cool completely on wire rack. Store in refrigerator. Yield: 1 loaf.

Directions for gift card: Store Brazil Nut Sensation in refrigerator up to 6 weeks.

Above: Brazil Nut Sensation gives a tropical twist to the traditional fruitcake. With Sourdough Wheat Bread Starter, you may simply give the sourdough starter or divide the gift portion in half and bake one loaf of bread to send along with enough starter for another loaf. Both breads stay fresh in handsome wraps of fabric fused to freezer paper. Matching fabric decorates the jar of Sourdough Starter. (See "Christmas Workroom," beginning on page 140, for instructions.)

113

Above: Package cheese spreads with style in decorated terra-cotta pots. (For instructions, see "Christmas Workroom," beginning on page 140.) Here, Cheese Ball with Marinated Dried Tomatoes and Spicy Cheese Spread are wrapped in clear plastic tied with a bow and then nestled into the fabric-lined pots. (Holiday Cheese Spread may also be packaged this way.) A purchased gift bag holds the Pita Chips.

CHEESE BALL WITH
MARINATED DRIED TOMATOES

>   3   (8-ounce) packages cream cheese,
>   softened
>   1   (7-ounce) jar oil-packed dried
>   tomatoes, drained
>   1   clove garlic
>   2   teaspoons dried basil
> ½   cup coarsely chopped pine nuts or
>   almonds, toasted

Position knife blade in food processor bowl; add first 4 ingredients. Process until smooth. Cover and chill at least 3 hours. Shape ½ cup mixture into a ball; roll in toasted pine nuts or almonds, pressing gently to make nuts adhere. Repeat procedure with remaining mixture and nuts. Wrap each ball in plastic wrap. Chill. Yield: 6 (½-cup) gifts.

Directions for gift card: Store Cheese Ball with Marinated Dried Tomatoes in refrigerator up to 5 days. Serve with unsalted crackers.

114

CHEESE CHRISTMAS TREES

2 cups (8 ounces) shredded Cheddar
   cheese
1 cup butter or margarine, softened
½ teaspoon salt
⅛ teaspoon ground red pepper
2 cups all-purpose flour
½ teaspoon lemon juice
   Paprika

Beat first 4 ingredients at medium speed with an electric mixer; stir in flour and lemon juice. Fill a cookie gun or press fitted with a tree-shaped disc to shape trees; follow manufacturer's directions, pressing onto ungreased baking sheets. Bake at 325° for 15 minutes. Sprinkle with paprika. Store in an airtight container or freeze, if desired, for up to 3 months. Yield: 5½ dozen.

SPICY CHEESE SPREAD WITH PITA CHIPS

1 (8-ounce) package cream cheese,
   softened
1 tablespoon milk
1 clove garlic, crushed
½ teaspoon dried oregano
½ teaspoon chili powder
⅛ teaspoon ground cumin
   Paprika
   Pita Chips

Combine first 6 ingredients; spoon into ½-cup containers, and sprinkle with paprika. Cover and chill at least 8 hours. Give with Pita Chips. Yield: 2 gifts.

Pita Chips:

4 large pita bread rounds
⅓ cup butter or margarine, melted
⅛ teaspoon dried oregano
⅛ teaspoon chili powder
⅛ teaspoon ground red pepper

Separate each bread round into 2 pieces; cut each piece into 8 wedges. Place in a large heavy duty,

zip-top plastic bag. Combine butter and remaining ingredients; drizzle over wedges. Close bag, and shake. Place wedges on ungreased baking sheets. Bake at 300° for 30 minutes or until crisp. Cool completely, and divide in half; store in airtight containers. Yield: 2 (32-chip) gift bags.

Directions for gift card: Store Spicy Cheese Spread in refrigerator up to 1 week; serve with Pita Chips.

HOLIDAY CHEESE SPREAD

1 (10-ounce) package shredded sharp
   Cheddar cheese
1 (8-ounce) package cream cheese,
   softened
1 medium onion, finely chopped
2 tablespoons mayonnaise or salad
   dressing
1 tablespoon prepared mustard
1 teaspoon celery seeds
1 teaspoon garlic powder
1 teaspoon Worcestershire sauce
1 teaspoon hot sauce

Combine all ingredients in a large mixing bowl; beat at medium speed with an electric mixer until smooth. Spoon into ½-cup gift containers; cover and chill. Yield: 5 (½-cup) gifts.

Directions for gift card: Store Holiday Cheese Spread in refrigerator up to 1 week. Serve with crackers.

SUGAR-COATED PEANUTS

1 cup sugar
½ cup water
½ teaspoon liquid red food coloring
3 cups shelled raw peanuts

Combine all ingredients in a Dutch oven; bring to a boil. Reduce heat, and simmer, stirring often, 10 to 15 minutes or until liquid evaporates. Spread peanuts in a greased 15- x 10- x 1-inch jellyroll pan, and bake at 300° for 30 to 35 minutes, stirring twice. Store in an airtight container. Yield: 4½ cups.

JERK SEASONING RUB

1½ tablespoons sugar
1 tablespoon onion powder
1 tablespoon dried thyme
2 teaspoons ground allspice
2 teaspoons freshly ground black
   pepper
2 teaspoons ground red pepper
1 teaspoon salt
¾ teaspoon ground nutmeg
¼ teaspoon ground cloves

Combine all ingredients; store in an airtight container. Yield: ⅓ cup.

Directions for gift card: Rub or sprinkle Jerk Seasoning Rub on chicken and seafood before broiling or grilling.

MEXICAN SNACK MIX

1 (12.2-ounce) package shredded
   whole-wheat cereal biscuits
1 (12-ounce) can mixed nuts
1 (6.5-ounce) package pretzel twists
⅓ cup butter or margarine, melted
1 tablespoon chili powder
¾ teaspoon garlic powder
½ teaspoon ground red pepper
1 cup raisins
¾ cup semisweet chocolate morsels

Combine cereal, nuts, and pretzels in a large bowl; drizzle with butter, tossing to coat. Combine chili powder, garlic powder, and red pepper; sprinkle over cereal mixture, tossing to coat. Place in a 15- x 10- x 1-inch jellyroll pan; bake at 250° for 20 minutes, stirring every 5 minutes. Let cool; stir in raisins and chocolate morsels. Store in an airtight container. Yield: 15 cups.

SPICE MIX

2 oranges, thinly sliced
7 to 8 teaspoons whole cloves, divided
7 to 8 teaspoons whole allspice, divided
7 to 8 (3-inch) sticks cinnamon, divided

Place orange slices on a lightly greased wire rack; place rack on a baking sheet. Bake at 200° for 5 to 6 hours or until dry, removing slices as they dry. Using kitchen shears, cut slices into eighths.

Place ¼ cup orange pieces, 1 teaspoon cloves, 1 teaspoon allspice, and 1 stick cinnamon in a small zip-top plastic bag. Seal and store in a cool, dry place. Repeat procedure with remaining ingredients. Yield: 7 to 8 gift bags.

Directions for gift recipe card: For a warming winter beverage, combine 1 bag Spice Mix, 2 quarts apple cider, and 1½ cups pineapple juice in a Dutch oven. Bring to a boil; cover, reduce heat, and simmer 20 minutes. Pour mixture through a large wire-mesh strainer, discarding spices. Yield: 9 cups.

For a fragrant aroma, simmer 1 bag Spice Mix with 1 quart water.

For a marinade for ham, combine 1 bag Spice Mix, 1 cup orange juice, and 1 cup ginger ale in a heavy-duty, zip-top plastic bag; add cook-before-eating ham. Seal bag, and refrigerate 8 hours, turning occasionally. Bake ham according to package directions.

SOUTHWESTERN SPICE RUB

1 tablespoon cumin seeds
1 teaspoon coriander seeds
8 dried chiles, stemmed and seeded
1 tablespoon brown sugar
1 teaspoon ground cinnamon
½ teaspoon garlic powder
½ teaspoon salt
¼ teaspoon black pepper
¼ teaspoon ground red pepper

Cook cumin and coriander seeds in a small skillet over low heat, stirring constantly, 3 minutes. Combine seeds, chiles, and remaining ingredients

Above: Place dry mixes such as Southwestern Spice Rub and Spice Mix in sandwich-size zip-top plastic bags and slip them inside pouches made from paper-twist ribbon (see page 140 for instructions). Tie with raffia and a suitable "garnish"— a dried pepper for the Mexican Seasoning Mix, for example, or a cinnamon stick for the Spice Mix.

in an electric blender; process until mixture resembles coarse powder. Store in an airtight container. Yield: ⅔ cup.

Directions for gift card: Sprinkle Southwestern Spice Rub on chicken, beef, and pork before grilling, broiling, or baking.

MEXICAN SEASONING MIX

¼ cup dried onion flakes
¼ cup chili powder
1½ tablespoons salt
1½ tablespoons cornstarch
1 tablespoon ground cumin
1 tablespoon dried garlic chips
1 tablespoon crushed red pepper
2 teaspoons beef-flavored bouillon granules
1½ teaspoons dried oregano

Combine all ingredients. Store in an airtight container. Yield: ¾ cup

Directions for gift recipe card: To make beef taco filling, brown 1 pound ground beef in a skillet over medium heat, stirring to crumble; drain well. Stir in 1 cup water and 2 tablespoons Mexican Seasoning Mix; bring to a boil, stirring occasionally. Reduce heat, and simmer, uncovered, 20 minutes. Serve in taco shells. Yield: 4 servings.

Tips: You can make seasoning mixes and rubs 3 months in advance and store them in the freezer.

* Dry roasting or cooking seeds over low heat heightens the flavor.

* Orange slices may be dried in a food dehydrator.

* Before using dried herbs and spices, check for good color (no fading) and an aroma that's strong and not musty.

117

Above: Raspberry Vinegar is so pretty, you'll want to present it in a clear bottle to let the jewel-like color show. For a package topper that can later serve as an ornament, hot-glue silk holly leaves and berries to a miniature vine wreath and slip it over the neck of the bottle. Place Stir-Fry Sauce in a gift bag made from paper-twist ribbon (see "Christmas Workroom," beginning on page 140) and tie with drapery cord. Add chopsticks to hint at the sauce inside.

RASPBERRY VINEGAR

2 cups fresh raspberries*
2 (17-ounce) bottles white wine
    vinegar
2 (3-inch) sticks cinnamon
½ cup honey

Combine raspberries and vinegar in a nonmetal bowl; cover and let stand 8 hours. Transfer to a large saucepan, and add cinnamon; bring to a boil. Reduce heat and simmer 3 minutes. Remove from heat; stir in honey, and let cool. Pour through a large wire-mesh strainer into glass bottles, discarding raspberries and cinnamon sticks. Store at room temperature 2 weeks. Yield: 1 quart.

*1 (16-ounce) package frozen raspberries, thawed and drained, may be substituted. Yield: 3½ cups.

118

STIR-FRY SAUCE

    1 (15-ounce) bottle soy sauce
    1½ cups Chablis or other dry white
        wine
    ½ cup dry sherry
    ⅓ cup firmly packed brown sugar
    2 cloves garlic, cut in half
    2 tablespoons chicken-flavored
        granules
    2 tablespoons grated fresh gingerroot
    2 teaspoons black peppercorns
    1½ teaspoons sesame oil

Combine all ingredients; cover and refrigerate 8 hours. Pour through a large wire-mesh strainer into bottles, discarding solids. Store in refrigerator up to 4 weeks. Yield: 4½ cups.

Directions for gift recipe card: Marinate 1 pound chicken or pork strips in ½ cup Stir-Fry Sauce 30 minutes. Drain, reserving sauce. Cook meat in 1 tablespoon vegetable oil in a large skillet, stirring constantly, until done; remove from skillet, and drain on paper towels. Add 4 cups mixed vegetables to skillet; stir-fry 2 minutes or until crisp-tender. Combine 1 tablespoon cornstarch, ½ cup water, and reserved sauce; add to vegetable mixture. Cook 1 minute. Add meat, and cook until thoroughly heated. Serve over cooked rice. (Store remaining sauce in refrigerator up to 4 weeks.) Yield: 4 servings.

INSTANT POTATO SOUP MIX

    1 (13.3-ounce) package instant
        potato flakes
    1 (9.6-ounce) package instant nonfat
        dry milk powder
    ½ cup dried onion flakes
    ¼ cup dried parsley flakes
    2½ tablespoons chicken-flavored
        bouillon granules
    ¾ teaspoon celery salt

Combine all ingredients; store in an airtight container. Yield: 11 cups.

Directions for gift recipe card: Combine 1 cup Instant Potato Soup Mix, 1 cup milk, 1 cup water,

and ⅛ teaspoon pepper in a saucepan; cook over medium heat, stirring constantly, until thoroughly heated. Sprinkle with shredded cheese, if desired. Yield: 2 cups.

HOT PINEAPPLE SAUCE

    1 (12-ounce) jar apricot preserves
    1 (8-ounce) can crushed pineapple,
        drained
    ½ cup finely chopped sweet red
        pepper
    ¼ cup finely chopped green onions
    2 tablespoons finely chopped jalapeño
        peppers
    2 tablespoons balsamic or red wine
        vinegar

Combine all ingredients in a small saucepan; bring to a boil, stirring often. Reduce heat, and simmer 5 minutes. Spoon into a gift container; cover and chill. Yield: 1⅓ cups.

Directions for gift card: Heat Hot Pineapple Sauce in a small saucepan; serve with pork, ham, and turkey.

SNAP BRITTLE

    2 (10-ounce) packages miniature
        round buttery crackers
    1 cup dry-roasted peanuts
    ½ cup butter or margarine
    1 cup sugar
    ½ cup light corn syrup
    1 teaspoon baking soda
    1 teaspoon vanilla extract

Combine crackers and nuts in a large bowl; set aside. Combine butter, sugar, and corn syrup in a saucepan; bring to boil. Boil 5 minutes; remove from heat, and stir in soda and vanilla. Pour over cracker mixture, tossing to coat. Spread in a greased 15- x 10- x 1-inch jellyroll pan, and bake at 250° for 1 hour, stirring every 15 minutes. Pour onto wax paper, and let cool.

Break into pieces, and store in an airtight container. Yield: 10 cups.

Gifts Kids Can Make

CHOCOLATE CHIP TUB COOKIES

- 1 cup butter or margarine, softened
- ¾ cup firmly packed brown sugar
- ½ cup sugar
- 1 large egg
- ¼ cup sour cream
- 1 teaspoon vanilla extract
- 2 cups all-purpose flour
- 1 teaspoon baking soda
- ¾ teaspoon salt
- 1½ cups semisweet chocolate morsels
- 1 cup coarsely chopped pecans

Beat butter at medium speed with an electric mixer. Gradually add sugars, beating until blended. Add egg, sour cream, and vanilla, mixing well.

Combine flour, soda, and salt; add to butter mixture, mixing well. Stir in chocolate morsels and pecans. Divide dough into 2 airtight gift containers. Yield: 2 (2½-cup) gifts.

Directions for gift card: Store dough for Chocolate Chip Tub Cookies in refrigerator up to 4 weeks. When ready to bake, drop by tablespoonfuls onto lightly greased cookie sheets. Bake at 375° for 10 to 12 minutes. Transfer to wire racks to cool. Yield: 2 dozen.

Note: Decorate 1-quart sherbet containers with stickers or sponge paint to use as gift tubs for cookie dough. Attach gift card with baking directions.

SPICE COOKIE MIX

- 1 (18.25-ounce) package spice cake mix
- 1 cup regular oats, uncooked
- ¼ cup firmly packed brown sugar

Combine all ingredients; store in an airtight container. Yield: 5¼ cups.

Directions for gift recipe card: Place Spice Cookie Mix in a large bowl; stir in 1 large egg, ¼ cup milk, ½ cup butter or margarine, melted, and 1 teaspoon vanilla extract. Drop by rounded teaspoonfuls onto lightly greased cookie sheets. Bake at 350° for 8 to 10 minutes. Transfer to wire racks to cool. Yield: 5 dozen.

FUDGE DROPS

- 1 (11.5-ounce) package milk chocolate morsels
- 1¼ cups granola cereal
- 1 cup salted peanuts
  Garnishes: candied cherries, candy-coated chocolate pieces

Place milk chocolate morsels in a microwave-safe bowl, and microwave at MEDIUM (50% power) 2 minutes. Stir in cereal and peanuts. Drop by teaspoonfuls onto wax paper-lined cookie sheets. Garnish, if desired. Chill until firm. Yield: 4 dozen.

CHRISTMAS CUPCAKES

- 1 (16-ounce) package pound cake mix
- ¾ cup milk
- 2 large eggs
- ½ teaspoon vanilla extract
- 1 (16-ounce) container ready-to-spread vanilla frosting
  Assorted candies

Combine first 4 ingredients in a small, deep mixing bowl; beat at medium speed with an electric mixer 4 minutes. Pour into paper-lined muffin pans; bake at 350° for 16 to 18 minutes or until a wooden pick inserted in center comes out clean. Remove to wire racks to cool. Spread tops with frosting, and decorate with candies, as desired. Yield: 16 cupcakes.

Note: To make chocolate cupcakes, add ¾ cup chocolate syrup to batter. Yield: 21 cupcakes.

Above: Each Christmas Cupcake will be a work of art when you turn your little chef loose. Provide a full "palette" of candies: peppermints, fruit leather, gummy bears, red-hot candies, and candy-coated chocolate pieces are just a few of the possibilities.

121

Above: Remember the candy Mom always used to make with marshmallow cream and crispy rice cereal? This Candied Cereal Pizza cleverly updates that old favorite. Package it in a pizza box that you decorate with paint and wrapping paper.

APPLESAUCE-SPICE MINI MUFFINS

1 (7-ounce) package apple-cinnamon
   muffin mix
½ teaspoon ground allspice
½ cup milk
¼ cup commercial applesauce
   Powdered sugar

Combine muffin mix and allspice in a large bowl; make a well in center of mixture. Add milk and applesauce, stirring just until dry ingredients are moistened. Spoon into paper-lined miniature (1¾-inch) muffin pans, filling three-fourths full. Bake at 425° for 10 to 12 minutes. Remove from pans immediately; sprinkle with powdered sugar. Yield: 2 dozen.

CANDIED CEREAL PIZZA

1 (10.5-ounce) package miniature
   marshmallows
¼ cup butter or margarine
¼ cup light corn syrup
8 ounces vanilla-flavored candy
   coating, finely chopped
1 cup dry roasted peanuts
6 cups crisp rice cereal
   Assorted candies

Combine first 4 ingredients in a large saucepan; cook over low heat until smooth, stirring constantly. Remove from heat; stir in peanuts and cereal. Let cool to touch. Spoon mixture onto a 12-inch pizza pan, and shape into a circle, slightly mounding sides. Decorate as desired, pressing candies into cereal mixture. Let cool completely; remove from pan, and transfer to gift box. Yield: 1 (12-inch) pizza.

Note: Present Candied Cereal Pizza in a real pizza box decorated in yuletide style. Unfold a 12-inch pizza box and lay it flat with the outside facing you. Coat outside with spray paint; let dry. Cut designs from holiday wrapping paper and attach to box with spray adhesive or glue. Refold box.

LITTLE BUCKAROO SNACKS

2 cups animal-shaped graham
   crackers
1 cup dry-roasted peanuts
½ cup candy-coated chocolate pieces
   or jelly beans
½ cup raisins

Combine all ingredients; store in an airtight container. Yield: 3½ cups.

HOT COCOA MIX

1 cup powdered nondairy coffee
   creamer
1 cup sifted powdered sugar
¼ cup cocoa
¼ cup mint chocolate morsels
½ cup miniature marshmallows

Combine all ingredients; store in an airtight container. Yield: 2⅓ cups mix.

Directions for gift recipe card: Add ⅔ cup boiling water to ⅓ cup Hot Cocoa Mix. Yield: 1 cup.

Note: Package mix in a plastic bag and give in a holiday mug with gift card attached.

Above: Give a friend the gift of a cup of hot chocolate every day for a week: One recipe of tasty, instant Hot Cocoa Mix will make 7 servings.

Desserts

KAHLÚA DESSERT

  1 (12-ounce) container frozen
      whipped topping, thawed
 ¼ cup Kahlúa or other coffee-flavored
      liqueur
1¼ cups chocolate wafer crumbs
  1 cup chopped pecans, toasted

Combine whipped topping and Kahlúa. Place 1 tablespoon chocolate crumbs in bottom of each of 10 (6-ounce) parfait glasses; top with ¼ cup whipped topping mixture. Repeat procedure. Sprinkle with pecans; chill. Yield: 10 servings.

Note: To serve dessert in 2-cup wine goblets, place 2 tablespoons chocolate crumbs in bottom of each of 5 goblets; top with ½ cup whipped topping mixture. Repeat procedure. Sprinkle with pecans; chill. Yield: 5 servings.

WHITE CHOCOLATE BROWNIES WITH HOT FUDGE SAUCE

  2 (6-ounce) white chocolate-flavored
      baking bars, coarsely chopped
  2 large eggs
 ½ cup sugar
 ¼ cup butter or margarine, melted
  1 teaspoon vanilla extract
  1 cup all-purpose flour
 ¼ teaspoon salt
  1 (6-ounce) white chocolate-flavored
      baking bar, coarsely chopped
 ½ cup chopped macadamia nuts or
      toasted chopped almonds
      Hot Fudge Sauce

Melt 2 chocolate bars in a heavy saucepan over low heat, stirring constantly. Remove from heat, and let stand 10 minutes.

Beat eggs in a small bowl at high speed with an electric mixer until foamy. Gradually add sugar, 1 tablespoon at a time, beating 2 to 4 minutes. Stir in melted chocolate, butter, and vanilla. (Mixture may appear curdled.) Add flour and salt, stirring until blended. Stir in remaining chocolate bar and nuts. Spoon into a greased and floured 13- x 9- x 2-inch pan. Bake at 350° for 25 minutes. Cool and cut into squares. Serve with Hot Fudge Sauce. Yield: 12 servings.

Hot Fudge Sauce:

 ⅔ cup whipping cream
 ¼ cup sugar
  1 (4-ounce) bar bittersweet choco-
      late, chopped
1½ tablespoons butter or margarine
1½ tablespoons light corn syrup

Combine whipping cream and sugar in a small heavy saucepan; cook over low heat, stirring constantly, until sugar dissolves. Add chocolate, stirring until chocolate melts. Stir in butter and corn syrup, stirring until butter melts. Yield: 1⅓ cups.

LUSCIOUS LEMON CAKE

1 cup shortening
2 cups sugar
4 large eggs
2 cups self-rising flour
1 cup all-purpose flour
1 cup milk
1 teaspoon vanilla extract
1 teaspoon lemon extract
   Lemon Filling
   White Frosting

Beat shortening at medium speed with an electric mixer until fluffy; gradually add sugar, beating well. Add eggs, 1 at a time, beating after each addition.

Add flours to shortening mixture alternately with milk, beginning and ending with flour. Mix after each addition. Stir in flavorings.

Pour batter into 4 greased and floured 9-inch round cakepans. Bake at 350° for 15 to 18 minutes or until a wooden pick inserted in center comes out clean. Cool in pans on wire racks 10

124

minutes; remove from pans, and let cool completely on wire racks. Spread Lemon Filling between layers; spread White Frosting on top and sides of cake. Yield: 1 (4-layer) cake.

Lemon Filling:

    1 tablespoon grated lemon rind
    ¼ cup lemon juice
    2 tablespoons water
    1 cup sugar
    ¼ cup butter or margarine
    4 large eggs, lightly beaten

Combine all ingredients in top of a double boiler; cook over boiling water 5 to 7 minutes, stirring constantly, or until thickened. Remove from heat; place plastic wrap directly onto top of filling to keep skin from forming. Cool. Yield: 1⅓ cups.

White Frosting:

    ⅓ cup butter or margarine, softened
    ⅓ cup milk
    1 teaspoon vanilla extract
    6 cups sifted powdered sugar

Cream butter at medium speed with an electric mixer. Combine milk and vanilla; gradually add sugar and milk mixture alternately to butter, beating after each addition. Add additional milk, if needed. Yield: 3 cups.

TWO-TONE POUND CAKE

    1¼ cups butter or margarine, softened
    2½ cups sugar
    5 large eggs
    2⅔ cups all-purpose flour
    1¼ teaspoons baking powder
    ½ teaspoon salt
    1 cup milk
    2 teaspoons vanilla extract
    ¼ cup cocoa
        Sifted powdered sugar

Beat butter at medium speed with an electric mixer about 2 minutes or until soft and creamy.

Above: Can't choose between chocolate and vanilla? Two-Tone Pound Cake offers the best of both. Sift powdered sugar over the top for a snowy effect.

Gradually add sugar, beating at medium speed 5 to 7 minutes. Add eggs, 1 at a time, beating just until yellow disappears.

Combine flour, baking powder, and salt; add to butter mixture alternately with milk, beginning and ending with flour mixture. Mix at low speed after each addition just until blended. Stir in vanilla. Remove 2 cups batter, and stir in cocoa. Spoon one-third of remaining batter into a greased and floured 13-cup Bundt pan; top with half of chocolate batter. Repeat layers, ending with plain batter. Gently swirl batter with a knife. Bake at 325° for 1 hour and 5 minutes or until a wooden pick inserted in center comes out clean. Cool in pan on a wire rack 10 minutes; remove from pan, and let cool completely on a wire rack (outer edge may stick to pan). Sprinkle with powdered sugar. Yield: 1 (10-inch) cake.

Above: For the taste of tradition without the fuss of a pie, serve bite-size Mincemeat Tartlettes with Brandy Hard Sauce at your next holiday buffet. You can whip them up quickly, using miniature puff pastry shells, commercial mincemeat, and a dash of brandy.

MINCEMEAT TARTLETTES WITH BRANDY HARD SAUCE

    2 (9-ounce) packages frozen
         miniature puff pastry shells
 1½ cups commercial mincemeat
    2 tablespoons brandy
         Brandy Hard Sauce

Bake pastry shells according to package directions; set aside. Combine mincemeat and brandy; spoon into pastry shells. Dollop with Brandy Hard Sauce. Yield: 48 tartlettes.

Brandy Hard Sauce:

    1 cup sifted powdered sugar
  ½ cup butter or margarine, softened
    2 tablespoons brandy
    1 teaspoon lemon juice

Combine all ingredients, and beat at medium speed with an electric mixer until light and fluffy. Yield: 1 cup.

CHOCOLATE-COFFEE ICE-CREAM TORTE

    6 soft coconut macaroon cookies,
         crumbled
    2 tablespoons butter or margarine,
         melted
    1 quart chocolate ice cream, softened
  ½ cup chocolate syrup, divided
    4 (1.4-ounce) English toffee-flavored
         candy bars, crushed and divided
    1 quart coffee or vanilla ice cream,
         softened

Combine cookie crumbs and butter; press firmly over bottom of a 9-inch springform pan. Spread chocolate ice cream over crust; drizzle with half of chocolate syrup, and sprinkle with half of crushed candy. Freeze until firm. Spread coffee or vanilla ice cream over crushed candy; drizzle with remaining chocolate syrup, and sprinkle with remaining crushed candy. Cover and freeze. Yield: 12 servings.

ALMOND CRÊPES

1 cup sugar
¼ cup all-purpose flour
1 cup milk
3 large eggs, beaten
3 tablespoons butter or margarine
1 teaspoon vanilla extract
¼ teaspoon almond extract
  Crêpes
1 (21-ounce) can cherry pie filling
2 tablespoons amaretto or other
  almond-flavored liqueur
  (optional)
½ cup slivered almonds, toasted and
  chopped

Combine sugar and flour in a heavy saucepan; stir in milk. Cook over medium heat, stirring constantly, until thickened (about 8 minutes). Gradually stir about one-fourth of hot mixture into beaten eggs; add to remaining hot mixture, stirring constantly. Cook over medium heat 3 to 4 minutes or until thickened. Stir in butter and flavorings. Cool.

Spread about 2 tablespoons custard mixture on each of 12 crêpes, and roll up. Place 2 crêpes on each dessert plate.

Combine cherry pie filling and amaretto, if desired; spoon evenly over crêpes, and sprinkle with almonds. Yield: 6 servings.

Crêpes:

1 cup all-purpose flour
¼ teaspoon salt
1¼ cups milk
2 large eggs
2 tablespoons butter or margarine,
  melted
  Vegetable oil

Combine first 3 ingredients; beat at medium speed with an electric mixer until smooth. Add eggs, and beat well; stir in butter. Cover and refrigerate 1 hour.

Brush bottom of a 6-inch crêpe pan or heavy skillet lightly with oil; place over medium heat until just hot, but not smoking. Pour 2 tablespoons batter into pan; quickly tilt pan in all directions so batter covers pan with a thin film. Cook about 1 minute or until crêpe can be shaken loose from pan. Flip crêpe, and cook about 30 seconds.

Transfer crêpe to wax paper to cool. Repeat procedure until all batter is used. Stack crêpes between layers of wax paper to prevent sticking. Yield: 14 (6-inch) crêpes.

DARK CHOCOLATE DECADENCE

1 (9-ounce) package chocolate wafers,
  crushed
1 (3.5-ounce) can flaked coconut
  (1⅓ cups)
⅓ cup butter or margarine, melted
¼ cup butter or margarine, softened
¾ cup firmly packed brown sugar
3 large eggs
2 teaspoons instant coffee granules
2 tablespoons hot water
1 (12-ounce) package semisweet
  chocolate morsels, melted
¼ cup all-purpose flour
1 cup cashews, coarsely chopped
1 cup whipping cream, whipped
  Garnish: chopped cashews

Combine chocolate wafer crumbs and coconut; stir in ⅓ cup melted butter. Press in bottom and 1 inch up sides of a lightly greased 9-inch springform pan.

Beat ¼ cup butter at medium speed with an electric mixer until creamy; gradually add sugar, mixing until well blended. Add eggs, 1 at a time, mixing only until yellow disappears.

Dissolve coffee in hot water; add to butter mixture. Stir in chocolate morsels, flour, and cashews. Spoon into prepared crust, and bake at 375° for 25 minutes. (Wooden pick inserted in center will not come out clean.) Cool on a wire rack. Chill 8 hours.

Dollop whipped cream around outer edge, and garnish, if desired. Yield: 1 (10-inch) dessert.

Warm, chewy Cheesy Pretzel Rolls make
a great snack after a long day of shopping.
Start with packaged hot roll mix and finish with your
choice of toppings—bake them with
a sprinkling of salt, sesame seeds,
or poppy seeds and serve with
hot mustard or cream cheese.

Breads

CHEESY PRETZEL ROLLS

  1 (16-ounce) package hot roll mix
      with yeast packet
 ½ cup (2 ounces) shredded sharp
      Cheddar cheese
  1 cup hot water (120° to 130°)
  1 large egg
  2 tablespoons butter or margarine,
      softened
  1 large egg, lightly beaten
      Kosher salt, sesame seeds, or poppy
      seeds (optional)

Combine hot roll mix, yeast packet, and cheese; add water, 1 egg, and butter, stirring until blended. Turn dough out onto a lightly floured surface, and knead 5 minutes or until smooth. Cover and let rest 5 minutes.

  Cut dough into 24 pieces; roll each piece on a lightly floured surface into a 9-inch rope. Twist into a pretzel shape. Place on lightly greased baking sheets. Brush with beaten egg, and sprinkle with salt, sesame seeds, or poppy seeds, if desired. Bake at 400° for 12 to 14 minutes or until golden brown. Serve warm. Yield: 2 dozen.

CREAM CHEESE BISCUITS

2½ cups self-rising soft wheat
      flour
  1 (3-ounce) package cream
      cheese
 ¼ cup butter or margarine
 ¾ cup milk

Place flour in large bowl; cut in cream cheese and butter with a pastry blender until mixture is crumbly. Add milk, stirring with a fork, just until flour is moistened. Turn out onto a lightly floured surface, and knead lightly 4 to 5 times; roll dough to ½-inch thickness, and cut with a 2-inch round cutter. Place on lightly greased baking sheets. Bake at 450° for 8 to 10 minutes. Yield: 2 dozen.

FREEZER WHOLE-WHEAT BREAD

    3   packages dry yeast
    2¼ cups warm water (105° to 115°)
    1   cup milk
    ½   cup firmly packed brown sugar
    ¼   cup sugar
    2   tablespoons salt
    ½   cup butter or margarine, cut up
    3   cups whole-wheat flour
    6¼ to 6¾ cups all-purpose flour,
            divided
    1½ tablespoons butter or margarine,
            melted

Combine yeast and warm water in a 4-cup liquid measuring cup; let stand 5 minutes.

Combine milk and next 4 ingredients in a small saucepan; heat until butter melts, stirring occasionally. Cool to 105° to 115°. Combine yeast mixture, milk mixture, whole-wheat flour, and 1 cup all-purpose flour in a large mixing bowl; beat at medium speed with an electric mixer until well blended. Gradually stir in enough remaining all-purpose flour to make a stiff dough. Cover and let stand 15 minutes.

Turn dough out onto a well-floured surface, and knead until smooth and elastic (about 8 minutes). Roll dough into an 18- x 12-inch rectangle; cut into three 12- x 6-inch rectangles. Brush evenly with melted butter, and wrap each rectangle securely with plastic wrap. Stack rectangles, separating with additional layers of plastic wrap. Freeze up to 2 weeks.

To bake each loaf, remove from freezer; let stand at room temperature 2½ hours or until completely thawed. Roll up dough, and place in a greased 8- x 5- x 3-inch loafpan, pressing down gently to flatten. Cover and let rise in a warm place (85°), free from drafts, 1 hour and 15 minutes or until doubled in bulk. Bake at 350° for 30 to 35 minutes or until loaf sounds hollow when tapped, shielding with foil after 20 minutes. Remove from pan immediately; cool on a wire rack. Yield: 3 loaves.

HERBED ONION ROLLS

    3   tablespoons butter or margarine
    2   tablespoons finely chopped onion
    ½   teaspoon minced garlic
    ½   teaspoon dried oregano
    ½   teaspoon dried tarragon
    ½   teaspoon dried basil
    1   envelope dry yeast
    ¾   cup warm water (105° to 115°)
    1   teaspoon sugar
    1   teaspoon salt
    2   cups all-purpose flour, divided
        Melted butter or margarine

Melt 3 tablespoons butter in a small skillet over medium heat; add onion and next 4 ingredients, and cook, stirring constantly, until onion is tender. Remove from heat; let cool.

Combine yeast and warm water in a 1-cup liquid measuring cup; let stand 5 minutes. Combine yeast mixture, sugar, salt, and 1¾ cups flour in a large bowl. Stir in herb mixture and enough remaining flour to make a soft dough.

Turn dough out onto a floured surface, and knead until smooth and elastic (about 5 minutes). Place in a well-greased bowl, turning to grease top. Cover and let rise in a warm place (85°), free from drafts, 50 minutes or until doubled in bulk.

Punch dough down; divide and shape into 12 balls. Place in a lightly greased 8-inch square pan. Cover and let rise in a warm place, free from drafts, 30 minutes or until doubled in bulk. Bake at 375° for 20 minutes or until golden brown; brush with melted butter. Yield: 1 dozen.

MARMALADE COFFEE CAKE

    ¾   cup orange marmalade
    2   tablespoons chopped walnuts
    ¾   cup firmly packed brown sugar
    ½   teaspoon ground cinnamon
    2   (11-ounce) cans refrigerated
            buttermilk biscuits
    ⅓   cup butter or margarine, melted

Spread marmalade in bottom of a greased 12-cup Bundt pan; sprinkle with nuts. Combine brown

Above: Orange Bread is guaranteed to melt in your mouth—and it's easy to make, using refrigerated buttermilk biscuits. Sandwich cream cheese in each biscuit and then dredge them in butter, grated orange rind, and sugar. Bake in a Bundt pan.

sugar and cinnamon in a small bowl. Separate biscuits; dip in butter, and dredge in sugar mixture. Stand each biscuit on edge around pan, spacing evenly. Drizzle with remaining butter and top with remaining sugar mixture. Bake at 350° for 28 minutes or until golden. Cool 5 minutes on a wire rack; invert onto serving plate. Serve immediately. Yield: 1 (10-inch) coffee cake.

ORANGE BREAD

 ¾ **cup sugar**
 ½ **cup chopped pecans**
 1 **tablespoon grated orange rind**
 2 **(11-ounce) cans refrigerated buttermilk biscuits**
 1 **(3-ounce) package cream cheese, cut into 20 squares**
 ½ **cup butter or margarine, melted**
 1 **cup sifted powdered sugar**
 2 **tablespoons orange juice**

Combine sugar, pecans, and orange rind in a small bowl. Separate each biscuit; place a cream cheese square in center of one half, and top with remaining half, pinching sides together. Dip in butter, and dredge in sugar mixture. Stand each biscuit on edge in a lightly greased 12-cup Bundt pan, spacing evenly. Drizzle with remaining butter, and sprinkle with remaining sugar mixture. Bake at 350° for 45 minutes or until golden brown. Immediately invert onto a wire rack. Combine powdered sugar and orange juice. Spoon over warm bread. Serve immediately. Yield: 1 (10-inch) coffee cake.

Tips: Yeast breads are done when an instant-read thermometer placed in the center of the bread registers 190°.

* Quick breads and yeast breads may be frozen for up to 3 months.

* For a warm place for yeast breads to rise, put dough, covered, in a cold oven with a pan of hot water on the rack underneath.

PUMPKIN MUFFINS

    4 cups all-purpose flour
1¾ teaspoons baking soda
    1 teaspoon salt
    ½ teaspoon baking powder
2¾ cups sugar
    1 tablespoon ground cinnamon
    1 tablespoon ground nutmeg
    1 tablespoon ground cloves
1¼ cups raisins
    ¾ cup chopped walnuts
    4 large eggs, lightly beaten
2½ cups mashed cooked pumpkin
    1 cup vegetable oil
    1 cup water

Combine first 10 ingredients in a large bowl; make a well in center of mixture. Combine eggs and remaining ingredients; add to dry ingredients, stirring just until moistened. Spoon into paper-lined muffin pans, filling two-thirds full. Bake at 375° for 20 minutes. Remove from pans immediately. Yield: 3½ dozen.

Note: Muffins may be frozen up to 3 months.

BANANA-WALNUT BREAD

    ½ cup butter or margarine,
          softened
    ¾ cup sugar
    2 large eggs
    2 cups all-purpose flour
    2 teaspoons baking powder
    ½ teaspoon salt
  30 vanilla wafers, finely crushed
    1 cup mashed ripe bananas (about 3
          medium)
    ½ cup milk
    1 cup chopped walnuts, divided

Beat butter at medium speed with electric mixer until creamy; gradually add sugar, beating well. Add eggs, 1 at a time, beating after each addition.
Combine flour and next 3 ingredients; add to butter mixture alternately with bananas and milk,

beginning and ending with flour mixture. Mix at low speed after each addition. Stir in ¾ cup chopped walnuts.
Spoon batter into a greased and floured 9- x 5- x 3-inch loafpan. Sprinkle with remaining walnuts. Bake at 350° for 1 hour or until a wooden pick inserted in center comes out clean, shielding with foil after 45 minutes. Cool in pan on a wire rack 10 minutes; remove from pan, and let cool on wire rack. Yield: 1 loaf.

SOUR CREAM DOUGHNUTS

    1 package dry yeast
    ¼ cup warm water (105° to 115°)
2½ cups all-purpose flour, divided
    1 teaspoon salt
    ½ teaspoon baking soda
    ¼ teaspoon ground nutmeg
    ½ cup sugar
    1 large egg
    1 (8-ounce) carton sour cream
          Vegetable oil
          Powdered sugar*

Combine yeast and warm water in a 1-cup liquid measuring cup; let stand 5 minutes.
Combine 1 cup flour and next 4 ingredients in a large mixing bowl. Add yeast mixture, egg, and sour cream, stirring well. Stir in remaining flour; cover and refrigerate 8 hours.
Punch dough down; turn out onto a lightly floured surface, and knead several times. Roll dough to ½-inch thickness; cut with a 2½-inch doughnut cutter. Cover and let rise in a warm place (85°), free from drafts, 30 minutes.
Pour oil to a depth of 3 inches into a Dutch oven; heat to 375°. Fry 2 or 3 doughnuts at a time 1 minute on each side or until golden brown. Drain well on paper towels. Sprinkle with powdered sugar, and serve immediately. Yield: 22 doughnuts.

* ¾ cup sugar and 1 teaspoon ground cinnamon may be substituted.

132

Confections

HOLIDAY PEPPERMINT PUFFS

- ⅔ cup butter-flavored shortening
- ¼ cup sugar
- ¼ cup firmly packed brown sugar
- 1 large egg
- 1½ cups all-purpose flour
- ½ teaspoon baking powder
- ½ teaspoon salt
- ½ cup crushed hard peppermint candy

Beat shortening at medium speed with an electric mixer; gradually add sugars, beating well. Add egg, beating well.

Combine flour, baking powder, and salt; add to shortening mixture. Stir in peppermint candy. Shape dough into 1-inch balls; place on greased cookie sheets. Bake at 350° for 12 minutes. Transfer to wire racks to cool. Yield: 3½ dozen.

ALMOND MADELEINES

- 1 (7-ounce) package almond paste, chopped
- ½ cup butter or margarine, softened
- 1 cup sugar
- 5 large eggs
- 1 cup all-purpose flour
- 1 teaspoon baking powder
- ½ teaspoon orange extract
  Vegetable cooking spray
- 2 tablespoons butter or margarine, melted
  All-purpose flour
  Sifted powdered sugar

Combine almond paste and ½ cup butter; beat at medium speed with an electric mixer until blended. Add sugar, beating until smooth. Add eggs, 1 at a time, beating after each addition. Combine 1 cup flour and baking powder; gradually add to almond mixture, mixing well. Stir in orange extract.

Coat madeleine pans with cooking spray; brush with melted butter, and dust with flour. Spoon batter into prepared pans, filling three-fourths full. Bake at 400° for 8 minutes or until done. Cool in pans on wire racks 5 minutes; remove from pans, and let cool completely on wire racks. Sprinkle with powdered sugar. Yield: 5 dozen.

JAM-FILLED SNOWMEN

- ½ cup butter or margarine, softened
- 1 cup sugar
- 1 large egg
- 2 cups all-purpose flour
- ¾ teaspoon baking powder
- ¼ teaspoon salt
- 1 teaspoon ground cinnamon
- ¼ cup milk
  Sifted powdered sugar
- ⅔ cup seedless raspberry jam

Beat butter at medium speed with an electric mixer; gradually add sugar, beating well. Add egg, beating well. Combine flour and next 3 ingredients; add to butter mixture alternately with milk. Chill 1 hour.

Roll dough to ⅛-inch thickness on a well-floured surface. Cut with a 4-inch snowman cookie cutter, and place on greased cookie sheets. Use a 1-inch heart-shaped cutter to cut out a heart in half of cookies; place each heart in hand of snowman. Bake cookies at 375° for 5 to 8 minutes or until lightly brown around edges. Transfer to wire racks to cool. Sprinkle cutout cookies with powdered sugar. Spread solid cookies with raspberry jam; top with cutout cookies. Yield: about 3 dozen.

Note: Cookies may be frozen up to 6 months; thaw and spread with raspberry jam.

133

DOUBLE CHOCOLATE-PEANUT BUTTER COOKIES

1¼ cups butter or margarine, softened
2 cups sugar
¼ cup creamy peanut butter
2 large eggs
1 teaspoon vanilla extract
2 cups all-purpose flour
1 teaspoon baking soda
¾ teaspoon salt
¾ cup cocoa
1 (1-ounce) square semisweet chocolate, grated

Beat butter at medium speed with an electric mixer until soft and creamy; gradually add sugar, mixing well. Add peanut butter, eggs, and vanilla, mixing well. Combine flour and remaining ingredients; gradually add to butter mixture, mixing well. Drop by rounded teaspoonfuls onto ungreased cookie sheets. Bake at 350° for 8 minutes. Transfer to wire racks to cool completely. Yield: 9 dozen.

Note: Cookies may be frozen up to 6 months.

PEANUTTY CLUSTERS

2 cups sugar
1 cup evaporated milk
¼ cup butter or margarine
18 large marshmallows
½ cup milk chocolate morsels
½ cup semisweet chocolate morsels
1 (8-ounce) jar dry-roasted peanuts

Combine first 4 ingredients in a heavy 3-quart saucepan; cook over medium heat, stirring constantly, about 10 minutes or until a candy thermometer reaches 234°. Remove from heat, and add chocolate morsels. Beat at medium speed with an electric mixer until chocolate melts; stir in peanuts. Drop by rounded teaspoonfuls onto lightly greased wax paper; cool and store in an airtight container. Yield: 3½ dozen.

CARAMEL-PECAN CHEWS

2 cups sugar
1 cup light corn syrup
3 cups whipping cream, divided
1 teaspoon vanilla extract
3 cups chopped pecans

Combine sugar, corn syrup, and 1 cup whipping cream in a heavy Dutch oven; cook over medium heat, stirring often, until a candy thermometer reaches 230°. Stir in 1 cup whipping cream; cook, stirring often, until a candy thermometer reaches 230°. Stir in remaining whipping cream; cook, stirring constantly, until thermometer reaches 240°. Remove from heat, and stir in vanilla and pecans. Pour mixture into a buttered 13- x 9- x 2-inch pan; cool. Cut into 1½- x ½-inch strips; roll each strip in a 5- x 4-inch piece of commercial candy wax paper or wax paper, twisting ends. Yield: 12 dozen.

HARD-CRACK CHRISTMAS CANDY

2 cups sugar
½ cup water
½ cup light corn syrup
½ teaspoon strawberry flavoring
10 drops liquid red food coloring
1 tablespoon powdered sugar

Combine first 3 ingredients in a saucepan. Cook over medium heat, stirring occasionally, to hard crack stage or until a candy thermometer reaches 300°. Stir in strawberry flavoring and food coloring. Pour into a jellyroll pan dusted with powdered sugar; let cool. Break into pieces. Yield: 1 pound.

Opposite: Fill gift baskets with these old-fashioned Christmas treats: clockwise from left, Peanutty Clusters, Caramel-Pecan Chews, and Hard-Crack Christmas Candy.

TOFFEE-FLAVORED COOKIES

¾ cup regular oats, uncooked
½ cup butter or margarine, softened
½ cup sugar
½ cup firmly packed brown sugar
1 large egg
1½ teaspoons vanilla extract
1¼ cups all-purpose flour
½ teaspoon baking soda
¼ teaspoon baking powder
¼ teaspoon salt
4 (1.4-ounce) toffee-flavored candy bars, coarsely chopped (about 1⅓ cups)
¾ cup chopped almonds, toasted

Place oats in container of an electric blender; process until finely ground. Set aside.

Beat butter at medium speed with an electric mixer; gradually add sugars, beating well. Add egg and vanilla, mixing well. Combine ground oats, flour, and next 3 ingredients; gradually add to butter mixture, mixing well. Stir in candy and almonds. Drop by heaping teaspoonfuls onto greased cookie sheets. Bake at 375° for 8 to 10 minutes or until lightly browned. Cool slightly; transfer to wire racks to cool completely. Yield: 4 dozen.

FLORENTINE JEWEL COOKIES

1½ cups all-purpose flour
½ cup sifted powdered sugar
½ cup butter or margarine, cut into pieces
2 tablespoons whipping cream
2 teaspoons vanilla extract
¾ cup butter or margarine
½ cup sugar
¼ cup whipping cream
½ cup chopped red candied cherries
½ cup chopped green candied cherries
½ cup chopped candied pineapple
1 cup sliced almonds
2 tablespoons grated orange rind

Position knife blade in food processor bowl; add first 3 ingredients. Process until blended. Remove food pusher. Slowly add 2 tablespoons whipping cream and vanilla through food chute with processor running, blending until mixture forms a ball. Press into a 15- x 10- x 1-inch foil-lined jellyroll pan. Cover and refrigerate.

Combine ¾ cup butter, sugar, and ¼ cup whipping cream in a heavy saucepan; cook over medium heat, stirring often, until mixture comes to a boil. Boil 2 minutes, stirring constantly. Remove from heat, and stir in remaining ingredients; spread over prepared crust. Bake at 350° for 15 minutes or until golden. Cool in pan on a wire rack. Cut into bars. Yield: 6 dozen.

Note: Cookies may be frozen up to 6 months.

CRANBERRY BARS

1½ cups all-purpose flour
1½ cups quick-cooking oats, uncooked
¾ cup firmly packed brown sugar
¼ teaspoon baking soda
1 teaspoon grated lemon rind
¾ cup butter or margarine
1 (16-ounce) can whole-berry cranberry sauce
¼ cup chopped walnuts or pecans

Combine first 5 ingredients; cut in butter with a pastry blender until mixture is crumbly. Set 1 cup mixture aside. Press remaining mixture into bottom of an ungreased 13- x 9- x 2-inch pan; bake at 350° for 20 minutes. Stir cranberry sauce, and spread over warm crust. Combine nuts and reserved crumb mixture; sprinkle over cranberry sauce, pressing down gently. Bake at 350° for 25 to 30 minutes. Cool; cut into squares. Yield: 2 dozen.

CHOCOLATE-AMARETTO CREAMS

  3 (6-ounce) packages semisweet
      chocolate morsels
  1 (14-ounce) can sweetened
      condensed milk
  ¼ cup amaretto or other almond-
      flavored liqueur
  ¼ teaspoon almond extract
 16 ounces chocolate-flavored candy
      coating, melted

Combine chocolate morsels and condensed milk in a saucepan; cook over low heat, stirring constantly, until chocolate melts. Remove from heat; stir in amaretto and almond extract. Cover and chill 8 hours.

Drop mixture in ¾-inch mounds onto baking sheets lined with wax paper; freeze 1 hour. Roll into balls (mixture will be sticky), and dip in candy coating. Place on wax paper to cool. Store at room temperature. Yield: 6 dozen.

MINCEMEAT CRESCENTS

  ½ cup butter or margarine, softened
  1 (3-ounce) package cream cheese,
      softened
  1 cup all-purpose flour
  ¾ cup commercial mincemeat
  2 tablespoons sugar
1½ teaspoons ground cinnamon

Beat butter and cream cheese at medium speed with an electric mixer until smooth. Gradually add flour, mixing well. Shape dough into a ball; chill at least 1 hour.

Roll dough to ⅛-inch thickness on a lightly floured surface. Cut with a 3-inch round cutter; place 1 teaspoon mincemeat in center of each cookie, and fold 1 side over filling, pressing edges together with a fork to seal. Place on ungreased cookie sheets. Bake at 375° for 15 minutes or until lightly browned. Transfer to wire racks to cool. Combine sugar and cinnamon; sprinkle over cookies. Yield: 2½ dozen.

Note: Cookies may be stored up to 3 days.

DATE-NUT BITES

  2 large eggs
  1 cup sugar
  1 cup chopped dates
  1 cup flaked coconut
  1 cup chopped pecans
  1 teaspoon vanilla extract
  ¼ teaspoon almond extract
      Sifted powdered sugar

Combine eggs and sugar; beat well. Stir in dates and next 4 ingredients; spoon into an ungreased 8-inch square baking dish. Bake at 350° for 30 minutes. Remove from oven; beat mixture immediately with a wooden spoon. Let cool completely. Shape mixture into 1-inch balls, and roll in powdered sugar. Yield: about 2½ dozen.

Note: This recipe contains no flour.

EASY CHOCOLATE TRUFFLES

  2 (8-ounce) packages semisweet
      chocolate squares
  ½ cup butter, cut into cubes and
      softened
  ½ cup whipping cream
  2 tablespoons dark rum
      Sifted cocoa

Melt chocolate in a heavy saucepan over low heat; remove from heat. Add butter, stirring until smooth. Stir in whipping cream and rum. Cover and chill 2 hours or until firm.

Dust hands with cocoa, and shape mixture into 1-inch balls. Chill 30 minutes or until firm; roll in cocoa, and place in an airtight container. Store in refrigerator. Yield: about 3½ dozen.

Above: What could be more festive for a holiday luncheon or open house than Sparkling Raspberry Punch? This yuletide variation on sangría goes well with Cheese Christmas Trees (see page 115 for the recipe).

Beverages

SPARKLING RASPBERRY PUNCH

    2 (10-ounce) packages frozen
       raspberries, thawed
    1 (6-ounce) can frozen pink
       lemonade concentrate, thawed
       and undiluted
  ¼ cup sugar
    1 (33.8-ounce) bottle blush or other
       dry pink wine
    1 (2-liter) bottle raspberry-flavored
       ginger ale or ginger ale, chilled

Combine first 3 ingredients in container of an electric blender; process until smooth. Pour mixture through a large wire-mesh strainer into a large container, discarding seeds. Combine raspberry mixture and wine; cover and chill 2 hours. Just before serving, stir in ginger ale. Yield: 6 quarts.

SLUSH PUNCH

    1 cup sugar
    1 cup water
    1 (46-ounce) can pineapple juice
    1 (16-ounce) can frozen lemonade
       concentrate, thawed and
       undiluted
    1 (48-ounce) bottle cran-raspberry
       juice drink
    1 (2-liter) bottle ginger ale,
       chilled

Combine sugar and water in a saucepan; cook over medium heat, stirring constantly, until sugar dissolves. Combine sugar mixture, pineapple juice, and next 2 ingredients in a large container; freeze.

  Remove from freezer 1 hour before serving. Place in a punch bowl, and break into chunks; add ginger ale. Stir until slushy. Yield: 5½ quarts.

PARTY PUNCH

    3   tablespoons red cinnamon candies
    3   tablespoons sugar
    ½   cup water
    1   (46-ounce) can pineapple juice
    1   (2-liter) bottle raspberry-flavored
        ginger ale, chilled

Combine first 3 ingredients in a small saucepan; cook over medium heat about 5 minutes, stirring until candies dissolve. Let cool. Combine candy mixture and pineapple juice; cover and chill at least 2 hours. Just before serving, stir in ginger ale, and serve over ice. Yield: 3½ quarts.

MINT-PINEAPPLE REFRESHER

    1   (10-ounce) jar mint jelly
    2   cups water
    3   cups unsweetened pineapple juice
    ½   cup lemon juice
    1   (12-ounce) can ginger ale, chilled

Combine jelly and water in a saucepan; cook over low heat, stirring frequently, until jelly melts. Let cool. Stir in juices; cover and chill. Just before serving, stir in ginger ale. Yield: 7 cups.

STRAWBERRY-ROSÉ PUNCH

    4   (750-milliliter) bottles rosé wine,
        divided
    4   (10-ounce) packages frozen sliced
        strawberries, thawed
    1   cup sugar
    4   (6-ounce) cans frozen lemonade
        concentrate, thawed and
        undiluted
    2   (750-milliliter) bottles champagne,
        chilled

Combine 1 bottle rosé, strawberries, and sugar; cover and let stand 1 hour. Pour mixture through a large wire-mesh strainer into a punch bowl; stir in remaining rosé, lemonade, and champagne. Yield: 6 quarts.

HOT APPLE CIDER EGGNOG

    3   cups milk
    1   cup apple cider
    ½   cup whipping cream
    2   large eggs, lightly beaten
    ½   cup sugar
    ¼   teaspoon ground cinnamon
    ⅛   teaspoon ground nutmeg
        Whipped cream

Combine first 7 ingredients in a Dutch oven. Cook over medium heat 10 minutes or until mixture reaches 160°. Pour into mugs, and top each serving with whipped cream. Yield: 2 quarts.

CHOCOLATE MONKEY

    1   quart vanilla ice cream, softened
    ¼   cup Irish cream liqueur
    2   tablespoons dark crème de cacao

Combine all ingredients in container of an electric blender; process until smooth. Yield: 4¼ cups.

INSTANT COCOA-IRISH CREAM MIX

    2¾ cups instant nonfat dry milk
        powder
    1½ cups instant cocoa mix for milk
    ½   cup nondairy Irish cream-flavored
        coffee creamer*
    ½   cup sifted powdered sugar

Combine all ingredients; store in an airtight container. Yield: 4⅓ cups.
  To serve, place ⅓ cup mix in a cup. Add 1 cup hot coffee or boiling water, and stir well.

*For Instant Cocoa-Amaretto Mix, substitute amaretto-flavored coffee creamer.

Christmas Workroom
Gift Ideas

PAPER-TWIST GIFT POUCH
(See pages 117 and 118.)

For spice mixes, fold in half an 18" piece of 4"-wide paper-twist ribbon. Stitch close to each long edge. Insert zip-top bag containing spice mix. Fold raw edges of pouch to inside. Tie with raffia.

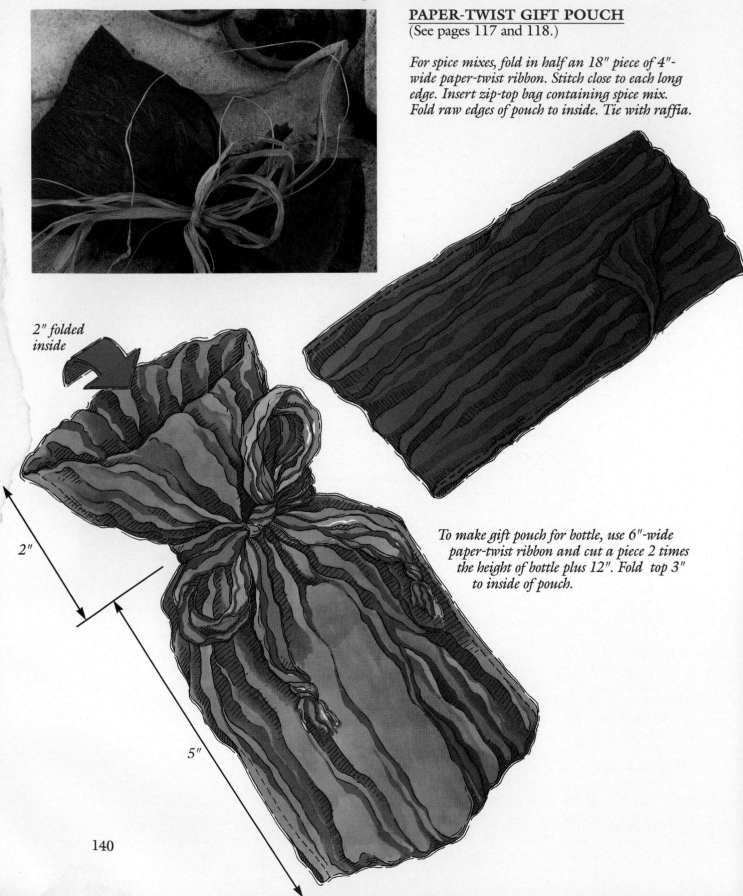

2" folded inside

2"

5"

To make gift pouch for bottle, use 6"-wide paper-twist ribbon and cut a piece 2 times the height of bottle plus 12". Fold top 3" to inside of pouch.

140

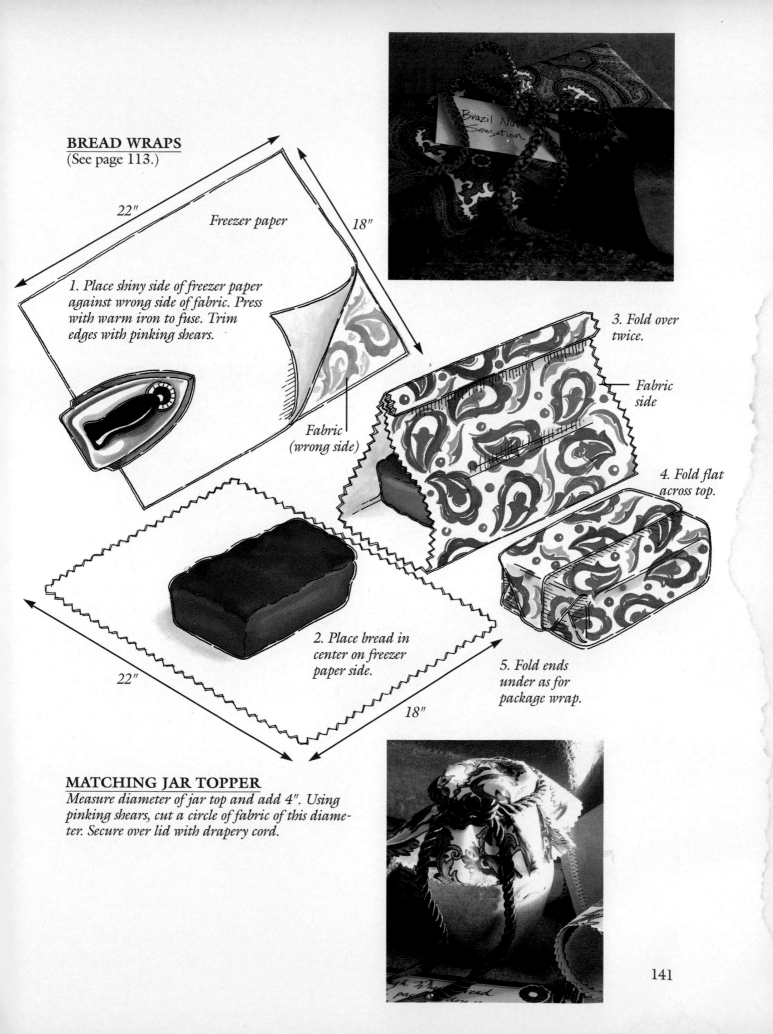

BREAD WRAPS
(See page 113.)

22"

Freezer paper

18"

1. Place shiny side of freezer paper against wrong side of fabric. Press with warm iron to fuse. Trim edges with pinking shears.

Fabric (wrong side)

3. Fold over twice.

Fabric side

4. Fold flat across top.

2. Place bread in center on freezer paper side.

22"

18"

5. Fold ends under as for package wrap.

MATCHING JAR TOPPER
Measure diameter of jar top and add 4". Using pinking shears, cut a circle of fabric of this diameter. Secure over lid with drapery cord.

141

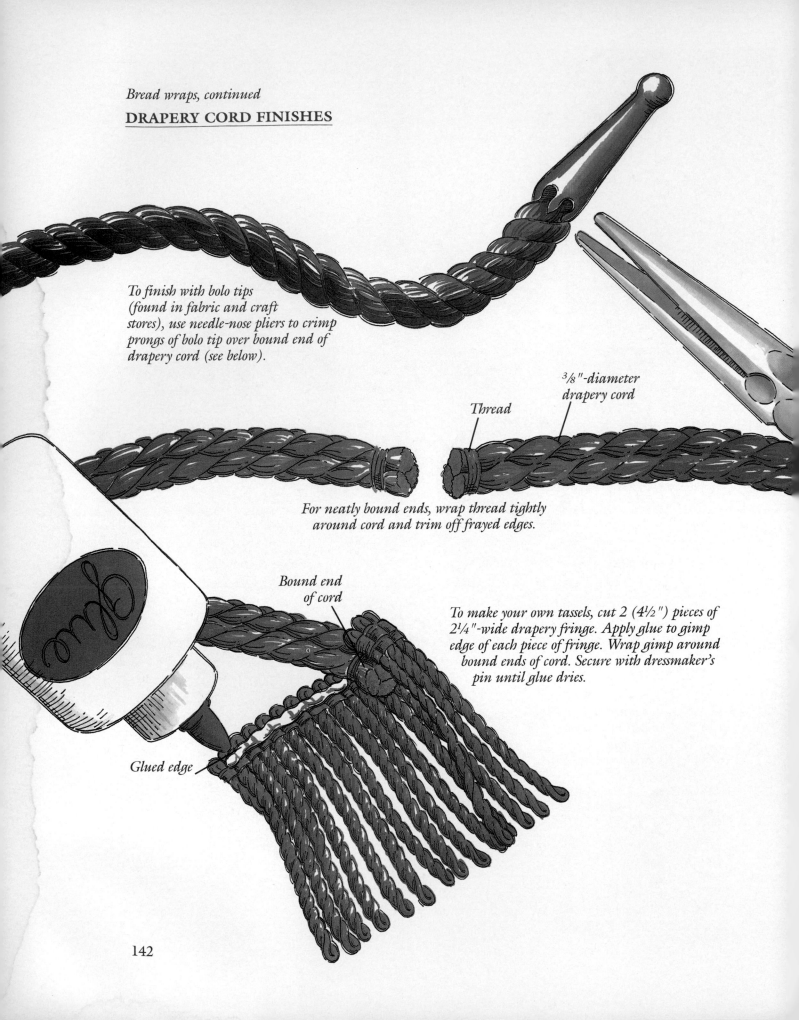

Bread wraps, continued

DRAPERY CORD FINISHES

To finish with bolo tips (found in fabric and craft stores), use needle-nose pliers to crimp prongs of bolo tip over bound end of drapery cord (see below).

Thread

3/8"-diameter drapery cord

For neatly bound ends, wrap thread tightly around cord and trim off frayed edges.

Bound end of cord

To make your own tassels, cut 2 (4½") pieces of 2¼"-wide drapery fringe. Apply glue to gimp edge of each piece of fringe. Wrap gimp around bound ends of cord. Secure with dressmaker's pin until glue dries.

Glue

Glued edge

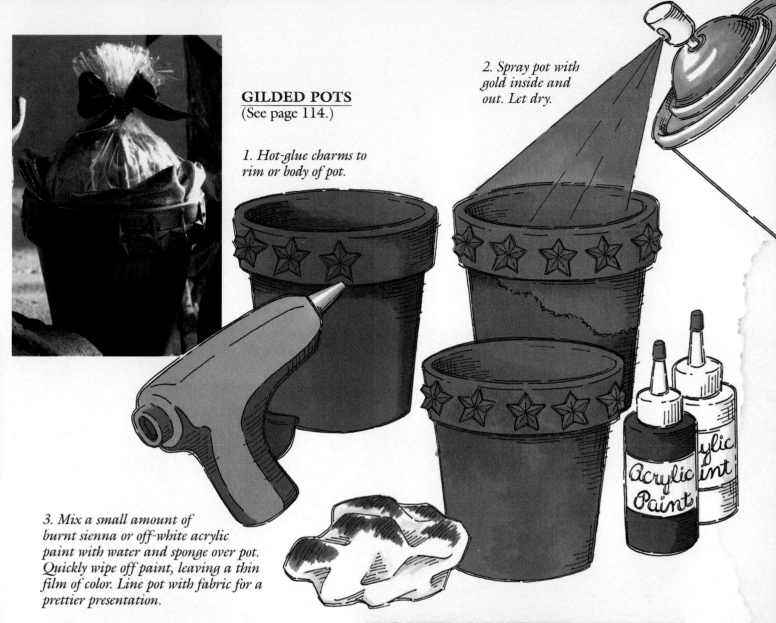

GILDED POTS
(See page 114.)

1. Hot-glue charms to rim or body of pot.

2. Spray pot with gold inside and out. Let dry.

3. Mix a small amount of burnt sienna or off-white acrylic paint with water and sponge over pot. Quickly wipe off paint, leaving a thin film of color. Line pot with fabric for a prettier presentation.

DRIED POMEGRANATES WRAPPED WITH GOLD
(See pages 96-97.)

Buy dried pomegranates or air-dry your own. Push in upholstery tacks to anchor the wire. Wrap fine gold or brass wire over and around fruit several times.

Badge Basics

(See page 59.)

Align stems of fir or pine branches. Wrap stems tightly with heavy florist's wire, forming a base.

Lay magnolia branches over fir and wire to base.

Continue adding greenery for desired full-ness. Hot-glue fruit in place.

Forcing Bulbs for Christmas

(See page 59.)

For narcissus: Fill pot to within 2" of rim with pebbles. Set bulbs into pebbles. Fill pot with water to just below base of bulbs. Keep pot in cool, dark place for several weeks. Keep water level just below base of bulbs. When shoots begin to grow, move pot to bright, indirect light.

For amaryllis: Fill pot to within 1 inch of rim with potting soil. Bury bulb so that half is below soil level. Water thoroughly, then place pot in bright light and do not water again until shoot appears.

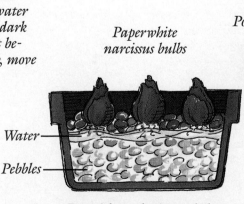

Amaryllis bulb

Potting soil

Paperwhite narcissus bulbs

Water

Pebbles

Pot without drainage holes

Drainage hole

144

Making a Garland

(See page 57.)

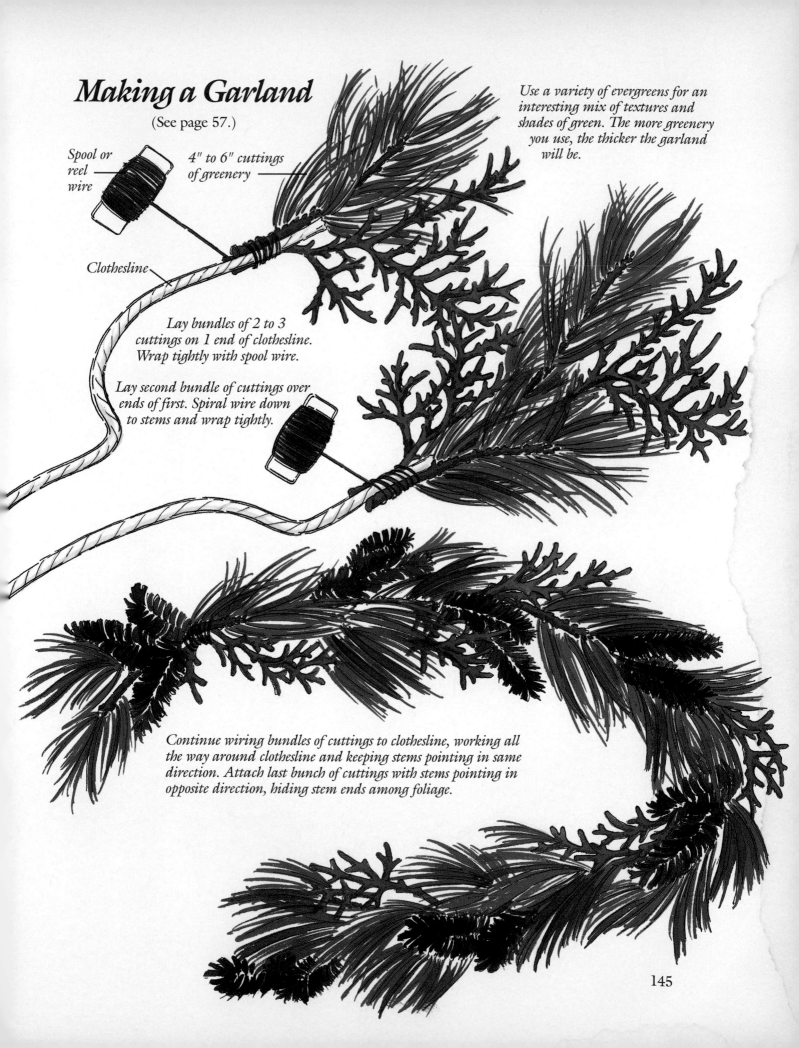

Spool or reel wire

4" to 6" cuttings of greenery

Clothesline

Lay bundles of 2 to 3 cuttings on 1 end of clothesline. Wrap tightly with spool wire.

Lay second bundle of cuttings over ends of first. Spiral wire down to stems and wrap tightly.

Use a variety of evergreens for an interesting mix of textures and shades of green. The more greenery you use, the thicker the garland will be.

Continue wiring bundles of cuttings to clothesline, working all the way around clothesline and keeping stems pointing in same direction. Attach last bunch of cuttings with stems pointing in opposite direction, hiding stem ends among foliage.

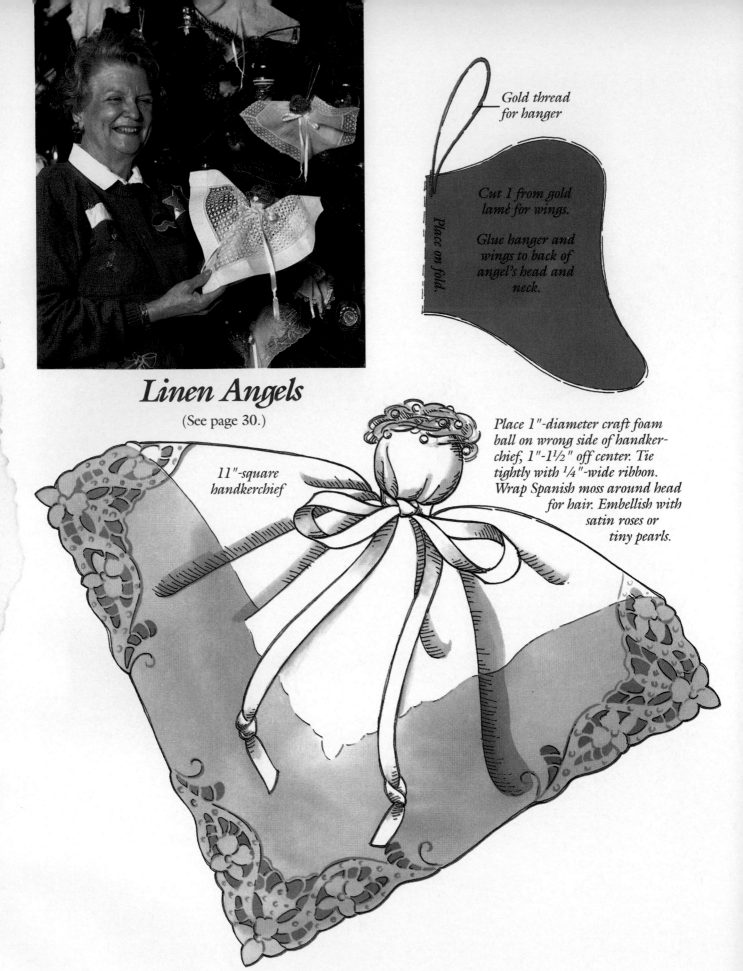

Gold thread
for hanger

Cut 1 from gold
lamé for wings.

Glue hanger and
wings to back of
angel's head and
neck.

Place on fold.

Linen Angels

(See page 30.)

11"-square
handkerchief

Place 1"-diameter craft foam
ball on wrong side of handkerchief, 1"-1½" off center. Tie
tightly with ¼"-wide ribbon.
Wrap Spanish moss around head
for hair. Embellish with
satin roses or
tiny pearls.

146

A Pineapple Newel from Savannah

(See page 56.)

Center a 4" x 4" x 2" craft foam block on top of an 8" x 8" x 2" block. Secure with 3" wood picks.

Cut 22-gauge florist's wire into 3" pieces and bend into U shapes to form pins. (Or use fern pins.) Using U-shaped pins, secure magnolia leaves in starburst pattern.

Lightly spray pineapple gold. Attach fresh, firm cranberries with U-shaped pins. Secure pineapple to craft foam base with 3 (7") wood picks. Add greenery to cover craft foam base. Accent with gold-painted twigs. Knot decorative cord around top of pineapple.

To make cranberry garland, thread firm cranberries onto 22-gauge wire. Twist ends together to make loop and wrap with florist's tape. Secure loops to craft foam with 3" wood picks.

147

Paper Collage Stars

(See page 60.)

*Enlarge pattern to 140% or draw stars freehand. Cut
from heavy watercolor paper.*
  Spray with gold paint and florist's glitter.
  *Randomly brush or sponge with silver and bronze inks
and draw fine lines to simulate marble veins.*
  *Write Christmas messages or carol verses with a
silver marker.*
  *Glue tinsel, stars, net, ribbon, painted papers
and scraps of shiny fabric onto the star.*

*Linda McIntosh
spread all of her
stars on a piece of white
cloth and then sprayed
them. She then used the sten-
ciled fabric for a window treatment, but points out that it
could also be used as a tree skirt.*
  *To give dimension to her stars,
she painted newsprint with wa-
tercolors and tore it into pieces,
then folded and pleated the
pieces before gluing them to the
star. "The secret is not to flatten
things out too much," she says.*

148

Potpourri Topiaries

(See page 66.)

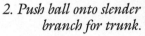

1. Coat craft foam ball with white glue and roll in rosemary. Let dry.

2. Push ball onto slender branch for trunk.

3. Loosely line clay pot with crumpled aluminum foil to keep pot from cracking.

4. Fill pot with plaster of Paris and insert trunk of topiary. Let dry.

5. Cover plaster with moss. Hot-glue nuts, holly, and cranberries in place.

Aromatic Bale

(See page 66.)

Coat craft foam block with white glue and roll in lavender or potpourri. Let dry. Wrap with gold crinkle wire, twine, or metallic elastic.

Patterns

Celestial Ornaments

Instructions are on page 86.
Patterns are full-size.

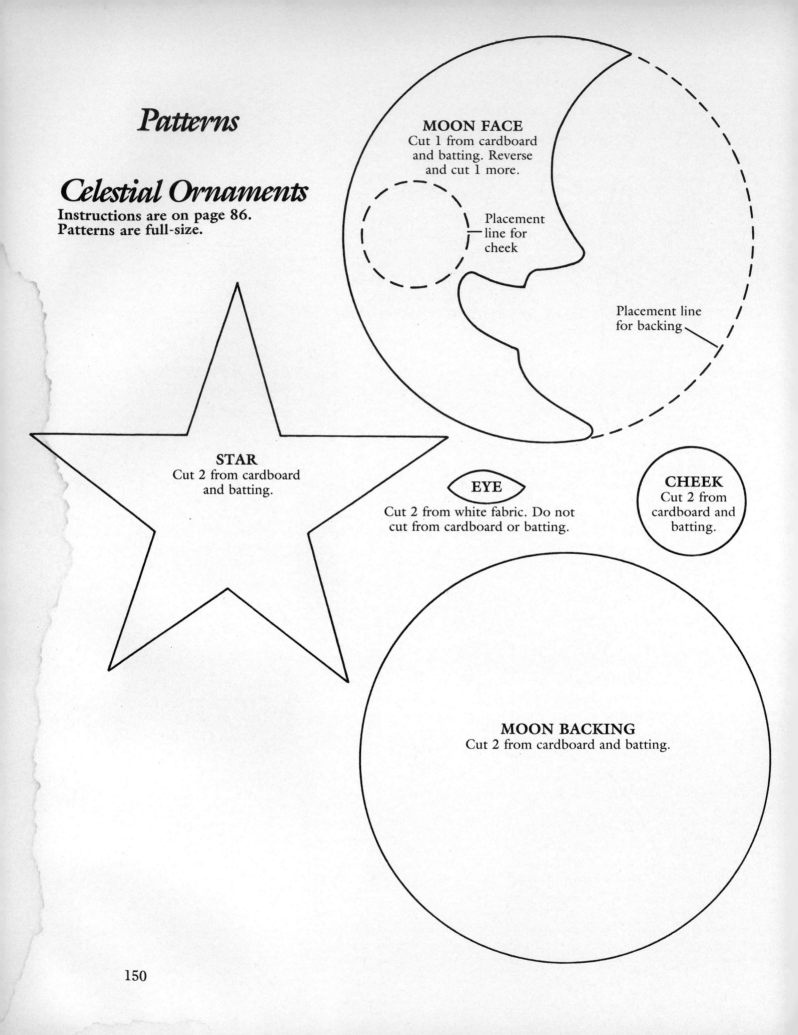

MOON FACE
Cut 1 from cardboard
and batting. Reverse
and cut 1 more.

Placement
line for
cheek

Placement line
for backing

STAR
Cut 2 from cardboard
and batting.

EYE
Cut 2 from white fabric. Do not
cut from cardboard or batting.

CHEEK
Cut 2 from
cardboard and
batting.

MOON BACKING
Cut 2 from cardboard and batting.

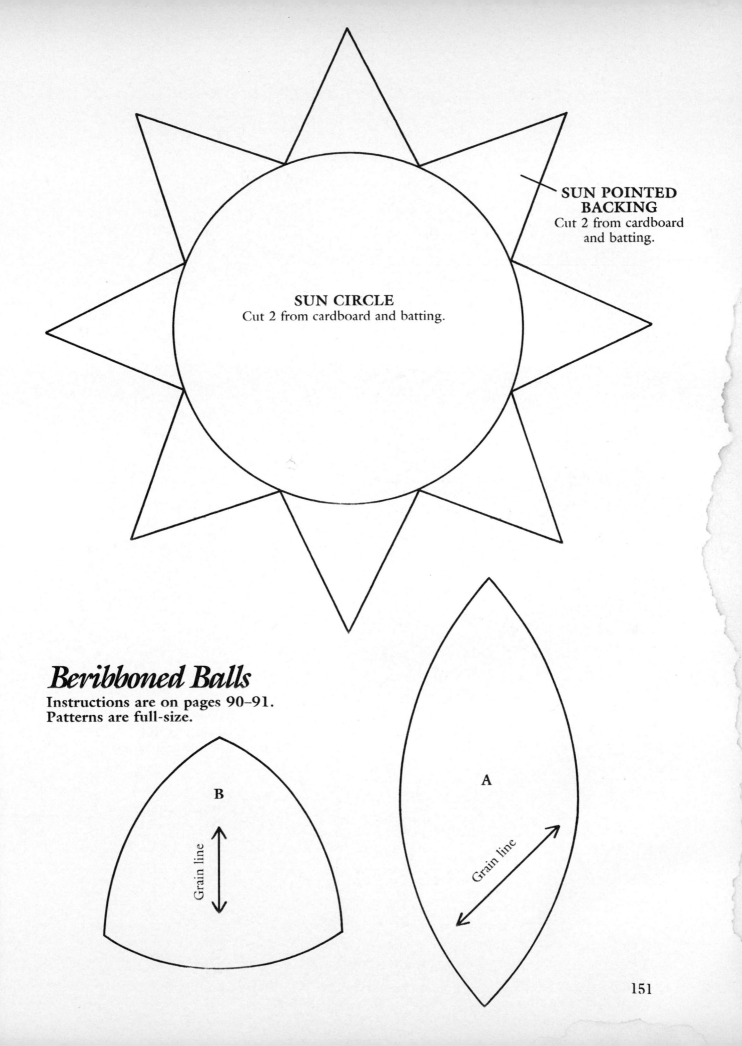

SUN POINTED BACKING
Cut 2 from cardboard and batting.

SUN CIRCLE
Cut 2 from cardboard and batting.

Beribboned Balls

Instructions are on pages 90–91.
Patterns are full-size.

B

Grain line

A

Grain line

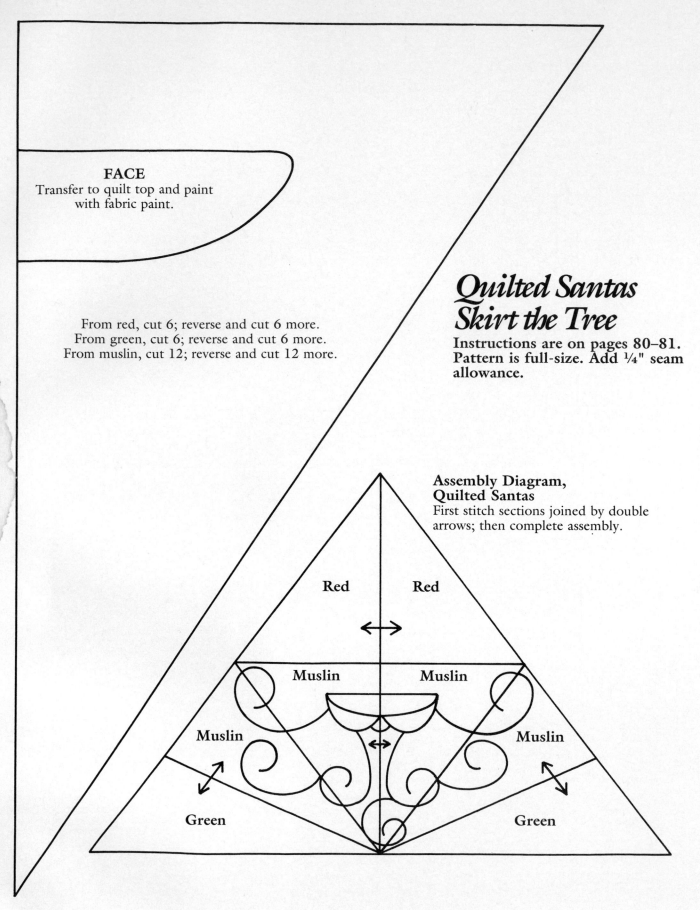

FACE
Transfer to quilt top and paint
with fabric paint.

From red, cut 6; reverse and cut 6 more.
From green, cut 6; reverse and cut 6 more.
From muslin, cut 12; reverse and cut 12 more.

Quilted Santas Skirt the Tree

**Instructions are on pages 80–81.
Pattern is full-size. Add ¼" seam
allowance.**

**Assembly Diagram,
Quilted Santas**
First stitch sections joined by double
arrows; then complete assembly.

Red   Red

Muslin   Muslin

Muslin   Muslin

Green   Green

Tabletop Angel

Instructions are on pages 93–94.
Patterns are full-size. All seam
allowances are ¼".

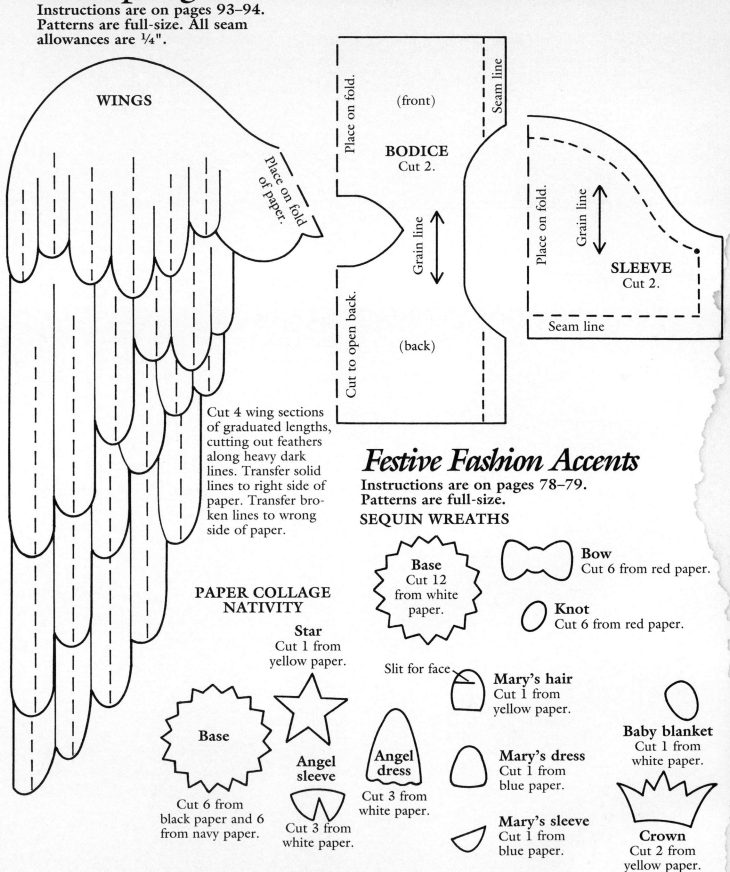

WINGS

Place on fold
of paper.

Cut 4 wing sections
of graduated lengths,
cutting out feathers
along heavy dark
lines. Transfer solid
lines to right side of
paper. Transfer bro-
ken lines to wrong
side of paper.

Place on fold.

(front)

Seam line

BODICE
Cut 2.

Grain line

Cut to open back.

(back)

Place on fold.

Grain line

SLEEVE
Cut 2.

Seam line

Festive Fashion Accents

Instructions are on pages 78–79.
Patterns are full-size.

SEQUIN WREATHS

Base
Cut 12
from white
paper.

Bow
Cut 6 from red paper.

Knot
Cut 6 from red paper.

Slit for face

Mary's hair
Cut 1 from
yellow paper.

Mary's dress
Cut 1 from
blue paper.

Mary's sleeve
Cut 1 from
blue paper.

Baby blanket
Cut 1 from
white paper.

Crown
Cut 2 from
yellow paper.

PAPER COLLAGE NATIVITY

Star
Cut 1 from
yellow paper.

Base
Cut 6 from
black paper and 6
from navy paper.

Angel
sleeve
Cut 3 from
white paper.

Angel
dress
Cut 3 from
white paper.

Candy Calendar
Instructions are on page 82.

Center

Center

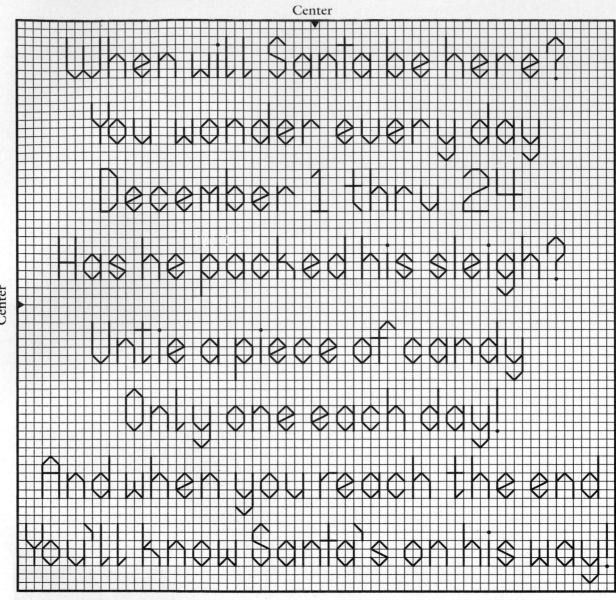

When will Santa be here?
You wonder every day
December 1 thru 24
Has he packed his sleigh?
Untie a piece of candy
Only one each day!
And when you reach the end
You'll know Santa's on his way!

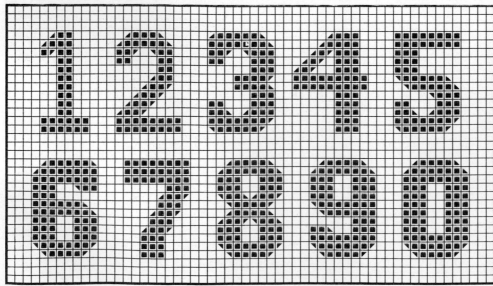

Color Key

⊞ 699 Green

(*Note:* Number is for DMC floss.) Backstitch verse using 3 strands of green floss; use 2 strands for numbers.

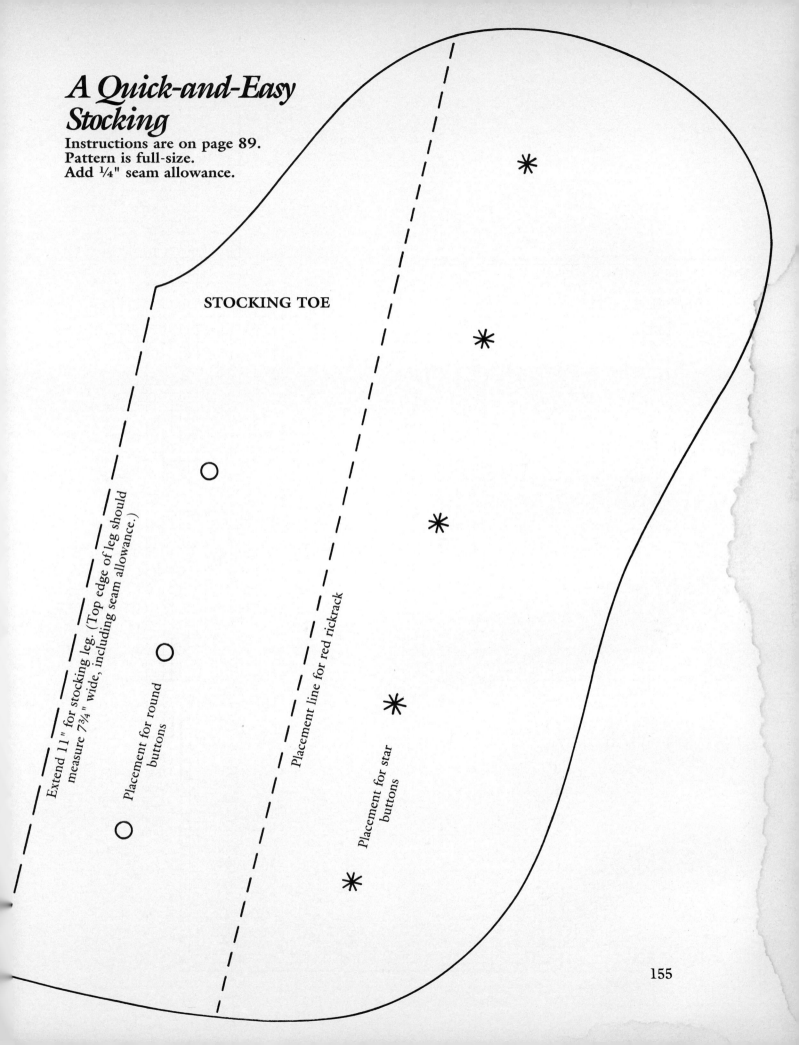

A Quick-and-Easy Stocking

Instructions are on page 89.
Pattern is full-size.
Add ¼" seam allowance.

STOCKING TOE

Extend 11" for stocking leg. (Top edge of leg should measure 7¾" wide, including seam allowance.)

Placement for round buttons

Placement line for red rickrack

Placement for star buttons

Contributors

DESIGNERS

Kelle Banks Barfield, knitted mitten stockings, 84–85.
Martha King Bonner, cross-stitch calendar, 82.
Kim Eidson Crane, ribbon-wreath nightshirt, 88; rickrack stocking, 89.
Charlotte Hagood, moss-covered baskets, 70–71; galax globe, 71; magnolia-leaf cornucopia, 72; lunaria pinecones, 72–73; lace-framed ornaments, 74; Christmas baskets, 83; beribboned balls, 90–91; tabletop angel, 92–94.
Françoise Dudal Kirkman, celestial ornaments, 86–87.
Dondra Parham, clove-studded stars, 61; puzzle purse greeting, 75; elf wreath, 76–77; button covers and earrings, 78–79; orange-and-cinnamon garland, 95.
Ginger Williams Rutland, quilted Santa tree skirt, 80–81.

PHOTOGRAPHERS

All photographs by **John O'Hagan** except the following:
Bill Cagle, 106.
Van Chaplin, 10–11, 19–21.
Colleen Duffley, 33, 96–101, 103, 105, 107–108 bottom left, 109 (right), 110, 113–14, 117–18, 121–23, 125–26, 128–29, 131, 135, 138.
Mary-Gray Hunter, 35, 84, 92.
Louis Joyner, 62–63.
Chris Little, 52–56, 67.
Hal Lott, 24–26.
Maxwell MacKenzie, 57, 59.
Sylvia Martin, 12–18, 30–31, 51 (except step 6), 64–66.
Beth Maynor, 36–39.
Larry Scaggs, 108 (top).
Melissa Springer, 28–29, 60.
Charles Walton, 102.
Donn Young, 111.

PHOTOSTYLISTS

All photostyling by **Katie Stoddard** except the following:
Bob Gager, 96–101, 107–110, 122–23, 125–26, 128–29, 131, 135, 138.
Leslie Byars, 113–14, 117–18.

RESOURCES AND ACKNOWLEDGMENTS

To join a tour of Yuletide at **Winterthur** and see holiday history for yourself, call 1-800-448-3883. Or write for information, ticket prices, and reservations c/o Winterthur Information and Museum Tours, Route 52, Winterthur, DE 19735.

For more information about **Old City Park**, Dallas, and the schedule of events for Candlelight, write to the Dallas County Heritage Society, 1717 Gano Street, Dallas, TX 75215; or call 214-421-5141.

For information and a schedule of Christmas Festival events in **Natchitoches**, write to the Natchitoches Area Chamber of Commerce, P.O. Box 3, Natchitoches, LA 71458-0003; or call 318-352-4411.

To make **Joy Jowell's garland**, write for a catalog and price list c/o Texas General Store, 2200-A Bayport, Seabrook, TX 77586; or call 1-800-982-9828.

For artificial lemons and leaves like those used on the **vine wreath** on the cover, call Jim Marvin Enterprises, Customer Service, 615-441-1015, for the name of the retailer nearest you.

To order **tin stars** or to find a retail source near you, write to Tin Originals, P.O. Box 64037, Fayetteville, NC 28306; or call 919-424-1400.

For a catalog of **stamping supplies** like those used to make the puzzle purse greeting card, send $5 to Personal Stamp Exchange, 345 South McDowell Blvd., Suite 324, Petaluma, CA 94954; or call 707-763-8058.

Many thanks to the following:
Mary Engelbreit for her card on page 32.
Terrafirma Ceramics, Inc., New York, New York, for the sauce dish on the cover and pages ii and 1.
The King's House Orientals, Inc., Birmingham, Alabama, for the use of the carpet on the cover and pages 2–3.
Handworks of Eastland, Texas, for the barbed-wire star and state-of-Texas ornament on page 2.
Winterthur Museum and Gardens, Direct Mail Dept. M 114, Winterthur, DE 19735 for the Winterthur Christmas Ball on page 3.
Jack Bowles of Irondale, Alabama, for the train schedules on page 2.
Rex Gustin of Eureka Springs, Arkansas, for the ornament on page 3.
Laurel Springs Fraser Firs, Laurel Springs, North Carolina, for the garland on page 51 and the wreath on pages 76–77.
Holiday Pine Christmas Tree Farm, Harpersville, Alabama, for the tree in the photographs on pages 32 and 80–81.
Special thanks to the *Southern Living* Test Kitchens staff for preparing recipes.
On page 96 and following, the china is Noritake "Tassel" and the crystal was designed by R. Guy Corrie for Union Street Glass, Oakland, California; the flatware is Gorham "Strasbourg."